DISCIPLE for LIFE.

Pursuing Holiness

APPLICATIONS FROM JAMES

Philip Nation

LifeWay Press® • Nashville, Tennessee

Editorial Team

Philip Nation
Writer

Reid Patton
Content Editor

David Haney
Production Editor

Jon Rodda
Art Director

Joel Polk
Editorial Team Leader

Brian Daniel
Manager, Short-Term Discipleship

Michael Kelley
Director, Groups Ministry

ISBN 978-1-4627-4285-1 • Item 005793401

Dewey decimal classification: 234.8
Subject headings: HOLINESS—BIBLICAL TEACHINGS \ BIBLE. N.T. JAMES—STUDY AND TEACHING \ SANCTIFICATION

To order additional copies of this resource, write to LifeWay Resources Customer Service; One LifeWay Plaza; Nashville, TN 37234; fax 615-251-5933; call toll free 800-458-2772; order online at LifeWay.com; email orderentry@lifeway.com; or visit the LifeWay Christian Store serving you.

Printed in the United States of America

Groups Ministry Publishing • LifeWay Resources • One LifeWay Plaza • Nashville, TN 37234

Contents

About the Author

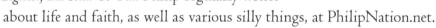

PHILIP NATION is the pastor of First Baptist Church in Bradenton, Florida. He is wildly in love with his wife, Angie, and constantly amazed by their two sons, Andrew and Chris. He's the author of numerous works, including *Habits for Our Holiness: How the Spiritual Disciplines Grow Us Up, Draw Us Together, and Send Us Out.* Philip regularly writes about life and faith, as well as various silly things, at PhilipNation.net.

Introduction

Jesus Christ saves us so that we can live lives of holiness. The concept of holiness is misunderstood, often interpreted in legalistic terms and rejected in favor of a desire to have more fun in life. But holiness isn't a way of life reserved for the most dedicated people of faith. It's the righteous standing all believers have before God because of Jesus' death and resurrection.

In this Bible study we'll walk through the Book of James to gain a more accurate understanding of holiness, and we'll learn how to align our thoughts and actions with the sanctifying work that Jesus has already accomplished for us. We'll discover that Jesus provides the empowerment and guidance for us to pursue holiness in our everyday decisions, circumstances, and interactions.

During this study we'll look at pursuing holiness in six arenas of life:

1. Wise and humble endurance
2. Obedience in real time
3. Relationships of grace
4. Putting holiness into practice
5. The way of humility
6. Powerful lives of prayer

My prayer is that you'll embrace the pursuit of holiness. It's not the natural tendency of the human soul. We normally pursue power, achievements, and pleasures. Through the transforming power of the gospel, however, Jesus leads us in a new way. We can pursue and live holy lives that declare the greatness of God, display the gospel of Jesus, and demonstrate the Holy Spirit's power in us.

How to Use This Study

This Bible study book includes six weeks of content. Each week has an introductory page summarizing the focus of the week's study, followed by content designed for groups and individuals.

GROUP SESSIONS

Regardless of the day of the week your group meets, each week of content begins with a group session. This group session is designed to be one hour or more, with approximately fifteen to twenty minutes of teaching and forty-five minutes of personal interaction. Meeting longer than an hour will allow even more time for participants to interact with one another.

Each group session uses the following format to facilitate simple yet meaningful interaction among group members, with God's Word, and with the video teaching by Philip Nation.

Start

This page includes questions to get the conversation started and to introduce the video session.

Watch

This page includes key points from the video teaching, along with space for taking notes as participants watch the video.

Discuss

These two pages include questions and statements that guide the group to respond to the video teaching and to relevant Bible passages.

Pray

This final page of each group session includes a prompt for a closing time of prayer together and space for recording prayer requests of group members.

INDIVIDUAL DISCOVERY

Each *Disciple for Life* small-group resource provides individuals with optional activities during the week, appealing to different learning styles, schedules, and levels of engagement. These options include a plan for application and accountability, a Scripture-reading plan with journaling prompts, a devotion, and two personal studies. You can choose to take advantage of some or all of the options provided.

This Week's Plan

Immediately following the group session's prayer page is a weekly plan offering guidance for everyone to engage with that week's focal point, regardless of a person's maturity level or that week's schedule.

Read

A daily reading plan is outlined for Scriptures related to the group session. Space for personal notes is also provided. Instructions for using the HEAR journaling method for reading Scripture can be found on pages 8–11.

Reflect

A one-page devotional option is provided each week to help members reflect on a biblical truth related to the group session.

Personal Study

Two personal studies are provided each week to take individuals deeper into Scripture and to supplement the biblical truths introduced in the teaching time. These pages challenge individuals to grow in their understanding of God's Word and to make practical application to their lives.

LEADER GUIDE

Pages 120–31 at the back of this book contain a guide that develops a leader's understanding of the thought process behind questions and suggests ways to engage members at different levels of life-changing discussion.

The HEAR Journaling Method for Reading Scripture

Daily Bible Reading

Disciple for Life small-group Bible studies include a daily reading plan for each week. Making time in a busy schedule to focus on God through His Word is a vital part of the Christian life. If you're unable to do anything else provided in your Bible study book during a certain week, try to spend a few minutes in God's Word. The verse selections will take you deeper into stories and concepts that support the teaching and discussion during that week's group session.

Why Do You Need a Plan?

When you're a new believer or at various other times in your life, you may find yourself in a place where you don't know where to begin reading your Bible or how to personally approach Scripture. You may have tried the open-and-point method when you simply opened your Bible and pointed to a verse, hoping to get something out of the random selection from God's Word. Reading random Scriptures won't provide solid biblical growth any more then eating random food from your pantry will provide solid physical growth.

An effective plan must be well balanced for healthy growth. When it comes to reading the Bible, *well balanced* and *effective* mean reading and applying. A regular habit is great, but simply checking a box off your task list when you've completed your daily reading isn't enough. Knowing more about God is also great, but simply reading for spiritual knowledge still isn't enough. You also want to respond to what you're reading by taking action as you listen to what God is saying. After all, it's God's Word.

To digest more of the Word, *Disciple for Life* small-group Bible studies not only provide a weekly reading plan but also encourage you to use a simplified version of the HEAR journaling method. (If this method advances your personal growth, check out *Foundations: A 260-Day Bible-Reading Plan for Busy Believers* by Robby and Kandi Gallaty.)

Journaling What You HEAR in God's Word

You may or may not choose to keep a separate journal in addition to the space provided in this book. A separate journal would provide extra space as well as the opportunity to continue your journal after this study is completed. The HEAR journaling method promotes reading the Bible with a life-transforming purpose. You'll read in order to understand and respond to God's Word.

The HEAR acronym stands for *highlight, explain, apply,* and *respond.* Each of these four steps creates an atmosphere for hearing God speak. After settling on a reading plan, like the one provided in this book in the "Read" section each week, establish a time for studying God's Word. Then you'll be ready to HEAR from God.

Before You Begin: The Most Important Step

To really HEAR God speak to you through His Word, always begin your time with prayer. Pause and sincerely ask God to speak to you. It's absolutely imperative that you seek God's guidance in order to understand His Word (see 1 Cor. 2:12-14). Every time you open your Bible, pray a simple prayer like the one David prayed: "Open my eyes so that I may contemplate wondrous things from your instruction" (Ps. 119:18).

H = Highlight

After praying for the Holy Spirit's guidance, open this book to the week's reading plan, open a journal if you'd like more space than this book provides, and open your Bible. For an illustration let's assume you're reading Philippians 4:10-13. Verse 13 may jump out and speak to you as something you want to remember, so you'd simply highlight that verse in your Bible.

If keeping a HEAR journal, on the top line write the Scripture reference and the date and make up a title to summarize the meaning of the passage. Then write the letter H and record the verse that stood out and that you highlighted in your Bible. This practice will make it easy to look back through your journal to find a passage you want to revisit in the future.

E = Explain

After you've highlighted your verse(s), explain what the text means. Most simply, how would you summarize this passage in your own words? By asking some simple questions, with the help of God's Spirit, you can understand the meaning of the passage or verse. (A good study Bible can help answer more in-depth questions as you learn to explain a passage of Scripture.) Here are a few good questions to get you started:

- Why was the verse or passage written?
- To whom was it originally written?
- How does the verse or passage fit with the verses before and after it?
- Why would the Holy Spirit include this passage in the Bible book?
- What does God intend to communicate through the text?

If keeping a HEAR journal, below the H write the letter E and explain the text in your own words. Record any answers to questions that help you understand the passage of Scripture.

A = Apply

At this point you're beginning the process of discovering the specific personal word God has for you from His Word. What's important is that you're engaging with the text and wrestling with the meaning. Application is the heart of the process. Everything you've done so far coalesces under this heading. As you've done before, answer a series of questions to discover the significance of these verses to you personally, questions like:

- How can this verse or passage help me?
- What's God saying to me?
- What would the application of this verse look like in my life?

These questions bridge the gap between the ancient world and your world today. They provide a way for God to speak to you through the specific passage or verse.

If keeping a HEAR journal, write the letter A under the letter E, where you wrote a short summary explaining the text. Challenge yourself to write between two and five sentences about the way the text applies to your life.

R = Respond

Finally, you'll respond to the text. A personal response may take on many forms. You may write an action step to do, describe a change in perspective, or simply respond in prayer to what you've learned. For example, you may ask for help in being bold or generous, you may need to repent of unconfessed sin, or you may need to praise God. Keep in mind that you're responding to what you've just read.

In this book or in your journal, record your personal application of each passage of Scripture. You may want to write a brief explanation-and-application summary: "The verse means _____ , so I can or will _____."

If keeping a HEAR journal, write the letter R, along with the way you'll respond to what you highlighted, explained, and applied.

Notice that all the words in the HEAR method are action words: *highlight, explain, apply, respond.* God doesn't want us to sit back and wait for Him to drop truth into our laps. God wants us to actively pursue Him instead of waiting passively. Jesus said:

> Ask, and it will be given to you. Seek, and you will find.
> Knock, and the door will be opened to you.
> **Matthew 7:7**

Wise and Humble Endurance

Week 1

Physical endurance has never been one of my strong points. As a teen-ager, I hiked. In my twenties and thirties I played racquetball. Along the way I've tried to be a runner. But I hate it. I pant and get a stitch in my side. Running makes my feet hurt, and I'm generally in a bad mood when it's all over. Whatever switch needs to be flipped in my psyche and in my body never seems to function. I just don't have the patience or endurance to be a runner. I've never been able to make the necessary adjustments to transition from amateur attempts to resolved runner. It's likely a combina-tion of bad form and bad attitude.

If we're to pursue holiness, it must become a greater priority than my attempts at running. Simply adjusting our behavior to present a better version of ourselves before God and others isn't enough. The Book of James helps us see that a walk of holiness is so much more than making exterior adjustments.

Holiness is a life that's completely devoted to the purposes of God. It's the way we can move from the attempt to be mannerly people to the total life commitment made by mature followers of Christ. As we pursue a biblical idea of holiness, endurance is essential, because life is going to get in the way of that pursuit. It won't be a breezy run down a comfortable slope. It's a challenging path that requires perseverance. Nevertheless, it's a race we run together as we're empowered by God's grace.

Start

Welcome everyone to session 1 of *Pursuing Holiness*. Use the following content to begin your group session together.

The Christian life can feel that it has a certain dual meaning. Jesus Christ paid the debt for our eternal salvation. Our position in Christ is established. It can't change. The moment we placed our faith in Christ, the Holy Spirit sealed us in a covenant relationship that will last forever.

At the same time, we now live out our salvation in a body that still desires the wrong things and in a world that's filled with temptations. These facts don't change our status with God, but they challenge our fellowship with Him.

Pursuing holiness can seem to be an odd concept because we're holy in our eternal standing with God as a result of our salvation in Jesus. Yet we must pursue a holy life every day because we live in a world broken by sin.

> **When you hear the word *holiness*, what images come to mind?**

> **As you begin this Bible study, what are your hopes for living a more focused life of faith?**

The first characteristic of holiness we will dig into is endurance. Endurance isn't exerting energy to make it on our own. Rather, it means accessing God's grace to live out the holiness we've already received through Christ.

We need wise and humble endurance. The world pelts us with commercials and products that promise to make us stronger men, independent women, and champions of all kinds. The gospel reminds us that we need holiness that's induced by grace, not by moral superiority.

Pray that God will open your hearts and minds before you watch video session 1.

Watch

Use the space below to follow along and take notes as you watch video session 1.

Holiness is something that happens in real life.

Holiness is how you've set your life apart.

Holiness requires endurance of all of your heart, your mind, your soul, and your strength.

Holiness is so much more than choosing between right and wrong. It is the choice to trust in Christ for His direction in everything that you're going to face, whether it's easy or whether it is the greatest hardship you think that you can endure.

Endurance is rooted in the work of Christ, not in your own personal strength.

Discuss

Use the following statements and questions to discuss the video.

When we think about holiness, we often think about a particular person or kind of person who seems to fit that concept. It might be a sweet grandma who always went to church and had a Bible by her bedside. Or it could be a monk who's hidden away from the temptations of the world. But holiness means a lot more than these images suggest.

What have been your usual definitions or ways of thinking about the concept of holiness?

Holiness is living according to the will and ways of God. But it's more than just making ethical choices. Holy living is born from the gospel's transforming work in us, and it's revealed in the way we live each day.

How would a more extensive definition of *holiness* change the way you relate to Jesus?

Read aloud James 1:2-8.

How can we turn our trials into joyful experiences?

James encouraged the first-century Christians to endure the difficulties in life by seeking God's insight. Living from God's revealed wisdom is a critical part of understanding life as God understands it.

In what areas of life—trials, temptations, or victories—do you need to seek God's wisdom to better understand your circumstances?

Asking for and receiving God's wisdom is an important step. But as we'll see, to progress in holiness, we must move beyond hearing to doing.

Choosing to live according to God's perspective instead of our own will require changes in both our thinking and our actions.

Read aloud James 1:19-27.

How can you make a deeper connection in your life between hearing the Word and obeying it?

What's one way you need to obey God's Word this week?

Many opportunities are available for us to hear God's Word, such as Bible studies like this one, sermons, personal devotional times, and podcasts. But the opportunities to obey the Word come at every moment of the day. James wrote to a group of believers who had to endure persecution while remaining faithful to Christ. He called them to hear God's Word and live it out, no matter the circumstances.

Why do faith and good works operate as companions for Christians?

Read aloud James 5:7-11.

Describe a current circumstance in your life that requires faithful waiting and endurance.

What changes would you like Jesus to make in your life in order to be glorified in you?

Endurance isn't just waiting but waiting with faith. A "Fake it till you make it" mentality won't suffice. Jesus is actively working in us so that we can rejoice in trials because they give Him more opportunities to increase our holiness. Endurance is rooted in Christ's work in you.

Conclude the group session with the prayer activity on the following page.

Pray

Conclude the group session by praying for yourself and group members in specific ways. Here are some prayer priorities to focus on before the next group session.

- Love for Christ that exceeds the joy you find in anything else

- Persevering faith no matter what trials you've recently faced

- Humility during times of testing so that your faith in Christ will grow stronger

- Strength to resist the temptation to become bitter or angry with people who offend you

- Faithfulness to Bible study and to a consistent prayer life that will draw you closer to God

Prayer Requests

Encourage members to complete "This Week's Plan" before the next group session.

This Week's Plan

Work with your group leader each week to create a plan for personal study, worship, and application between group sessions. Select from the following optional activities to match your personal preferences and available time.

Worship

[ ] Read your Bible. Complete the reading plan on page 20.

[ ] Spend time with God by engaging with the devotional experience on page 21.

[ ] Pray daily for the church and for group members.

Personal Study

[ ] Read and interact with "Trials and Our Maturity" on page 22.

[ ] Read and interact with "Enduring until the End" on page 26.

Application

[ ] Identify an area of your life in which spiritual growth isn't taking place. Invite a small group of believers (perhaps from your Bible-study group) to begin holding you accountable in this area.

[ ] Memorize James 1:4: "Let endurance have its full effect, so that you may be mature and complete, lacking nothing."

[ ] Start a journal by recording different ways you benefit from the ministry of the church. Specifically address how the church prepares you to endure trials and obey God faithfully.

[ ] List five other Christians you want to encourage to endure through their trials and temptations. Decide how you can actively encourage them over the next few weeks.

Did you miss the group session?
Video sessions available for purchase at lifeway.com/pursuingholiness

19

Read

Read the following Scripture passages this week. Use the acronym HEAR and the space provided to record your thoughts or action steps.

Day 1: Romans 5:1-5

Day 2: Galatians 6:6-9

Day 3: Psalm 100:1-5

Day 4: 2 Corinthians 4:16-18

Day 5: Daniel 3:13-18

Day 6: Psalm 121:1-8

Day 7: Hebrews 11:32-40

Reflect

LEARNING FROM THE PAST

Pursuing endurance seems to be an impossible task. If you need endurance, you often don't have much stamina. But you're called to a life of holiness that requires that you endure. So how do you get persistence and tenacity when you're struggling just to survive each day? Let's start with a challenge based on some encouragement:

> Therefore, since we also have such a large cloud of witnesses surrounding us, let us lay aside every hindrance and the sin that so easily ensnares us. Let us run with endurance the race that lies before us, keeping our eyes on Jesus, the source and perfecter of our faith. For the joy that lay before him, he endured the cross, despising the shame, and sat down at the right hand of the throne of God.
> **Hebrews 12:1-2**

The writer of Hebrews shows us what it looks like to endure through troubles. The first verse starts with *therefore*, signaling that a conclusion is being drawn from what came before this verse. Hebrews 11 is often called the hall of faith because it contains a long list of Old Testament examples of enduring faith.

We're often told to learn from our past. Many times the lessons are in negative form because we commonly learn from our mistakes. In contrast, the writer of Hebrews said to learn from the persistent faith of godly people who overcame life's toughest challenges.

Hebrews 11 presses us to remember the stories of Abraham, Noah, Sarah, Moses, Gideon, and others in the "large cloud of witnesses" (12:1). They were normal people who, when facing brutal challenges, chose to believe in a grace-giving God. Their faithfulness is a great encouragement for every challenge you currently face.

Personal Study 1

TRIALS AND OUR MATURITY

The idea that you can be happy when things go wrong seems unreasonable. But pursuing a holy life makes that possible To be holy means to be set apart or distinct. Our entire purpose as Christians is to be set apart from the way of life that seems normal to the world. In fact, God uses our trials to shape our Christian lives so that we grow more like Jesus and bring glory to Him.

Holiness is a state of life that comes with a cost. Our eternally righteous status before God cost: He gave His life on the cross in our place for our sins. Our own pursuit of holiness will also come at a cost. When we die to our old way of life, we're able to view life's circumstances very differently from the way the world views them.

Trials for Our Good

Unbelievers view calamities and may feel hopelessness or despair. In contrast, believers have a spiritual frame of reference that allows us to see trials and temptations through a new lens. This is why James wrote:

> Consider it a great joy, my brothers and sisters, whenever
> you experience various trials, because you know that
> the testing of your faith produces endurance.
> **James 1:2-3**

Identify a recent test that tried your patience in a relationship, a temptation to do something immoral, or an unexpected circumstance that could have led you to question God's good character.

In what ways did your trial present an opportunity for your faith to increase? Did it increase? Explain.

Counterintuitive is one of my favorite words. It means something is the opposite of what we expect. When we think about spending our lives pursuing holiness, we might expect life to get easier: *I'm doing the right thing, so only good things will happen to me.* But pursuing holiness is a counterintuitive lifestyle, especially when it comes with difficult circumstances. James teaches us that trials are designed to mature us in our faith.

Read James 1:4. What will endurance produce in a joyful disciple?

How do faith and endurance advance your maturity so that you'll be complete as a Christian?

Wisdom Granted

Endurance isn't done mindlessly. To persevere in the faith, you need wisdom.

What current circumstances in your life require greater wisdom from God so that you can navigate them with maturity?

Issues	*Answers You Need*

Read James 1:5-8.

James promises that God's wisdom is available to us. If that were all it said, we would walk away with gratefulness. But these verses promise so much more.

What if God made His wisdom available, but you had to fill out paperwork, make endless pilgrimages to mystics on mountaintops, and offer innumerable sacrifices to pay for it? You would be glad that it's available but likely frustrated that it was so hard to secure. All we must do to receive God's wisdom is to ask for it. The pursuit of a holy life is also the pursuit of an informed life. Knowing God's mind and heart will allow us to endure in our trials:

> If any of you lacks wisdom, he should ask God—who gives
> to all generously and ungrudgingly—and it will be given
> to him. But let him ask in faith without doubting.
> **James 1:5-6**

What are the only requirements to receive wisdom from God?

Circle the key words in the following verses that warn us about how not to seek God's wisdom.

> The doubter is like the surging sea, driven and tossed by the
> wind. That person should not expect to receive anything from
> the Lord, being double-minded and unstable in all his ways.
> **James 1:6-8**

God will grant His wisdom to any believer who asks in faith, but if we doubt that God will grant it to us, we'll miss out on what's available. Being determined in our Christian living is critical. God won't entrust the eternally precious gift of His wisdom to someone who's bent on wasting it. Instead, God desires to give wisdom to people who'll put it into practice.

What's the difference between someone who holds on to an enduring faith and the doubter described in James 1:6-8?

People with enduring faith can count on godly wisdom to guide them.

Bragging Properly

If you've navigated difficult trials by using heavenly wisdom, you may be tempted to brag about the way you handled your trials. But people who have pursued holiness must remember that any success they enjoyed came through the grace of God. We brag on God in humble gratitude.

Read James 1:12. What's the reward of a believer who endures trials?

This verse states that the people who receive the crown of life—the reward of eternal life—are the ones who love God. The importance of this promise can't be overstated. Our endurance in pursuing a life set apart for God must be birthed from love. We'll possess endurance only when we love God to the extent that we allow Him to reign in our lives.

Recognizing our weakness and our dependence on God puts us in a position to properly boast in His work in us. In pursuing holiness, if you regard trials as opportunities to fail, you'll likely do just that. Flip the script. Look at every test as an opportunity to reveal God's work in you. Commit your life to Christ as a showcase for His power. Then you can consider each trial with joy.

End your study today by placing your trial in God's hands and asking for His wisdom to endure in a way that brings glory to Him.

Personal Study 2

ENDURING UNTIL THE END

Endurance requires the proper motivation. When athletes train, they're motivated by the ideas of gaining victory over competitors or beating their personal bests. Musicians and other artists are motivated to produce great beauty in their craft. Motivations can also be negative, as when students or employees strive to succeed in order to avoid punishment.

What's the motivation in your life for common tasks like work and family responsibilities?

Throughout James's letter we consistently see that endurance finds its motivation in who God is rather than in who we are. Endurance isn't focused just on outlasting trials, temptations, and demonic attacks. Its true purpose is for us to know who God is and why we want to pursue a life that honors Him.

Learning God's Character and Ours

Trials, maturity, and understanding God's character are linked in James 1.

Read James 1:13. What's revealed about God's relationship with us by the fact that He's never tempted by evil?

How is your faith increased by knowing God would never lead you to do something unholy?

The temptations we face often begin internally. The old nature we still carry in our flesh has evil desires. We face plenty of external temptations in the world, but our own hidden desires are very strong. They present a progressive path for sin to take hold of our lives.

Using James 1:14-15, chart the progression from temptation to death.

To have enduring holiness, we must recognize the proper authority. Submission to God's reign will guide us to reject the rebellious longings of our flesh. But the opposite is also true: if we give in to the flesh, we'll displace God's reign. When we honestly face the scheming nature of our own flesh and recognize God's pure holiness, we'll happily pursue holiness with God's character as our strength and motivation.

Anticipating the End of the World

Follow God's heart and nature rather than our flesh gives us a long view of life. In fact, it helps us endure because we have eternity in mind. The shortsighted nature of the flesh wants us to consider only the pleasure we can have in the moment. God has much more in mind.

Read James 5:7-11. Underline the examples of endurance.

Brothers and sisters, be patient until the Lord's coming. See how the farmer waits for the precious fruit of the earth and is patient with it until it receives the early and the late rains. You also must be patient. Strengthen your hearts, because the Lord's coming is near. Brothers and sisters, do not complain about one another, so that you will not be judged. Look, the judge stands at the door!

Brothers and sisters, take the prophets who spoke in the
Lord's name as an example of suffering and patience. See,
we count as blessed those who have endured. You have heard
of Job's endurance and have seen the outcome that the Lord
brought about—the Lord is compassionate and merciful.
James 5:7-11

Which of the images for patience and endurance seems to connect most deeply with your life right now? Explain.

Athletes have a time clock or a finish line. Students have maximum scores and dates that end each academic year. Businesses have budget cycles. Parents know they have their children for only a certain number of years. What do Christians have as a motivation to endure? We know the Lord will return to bring a close to human history, according to His good plan. We endure while keeping in mind that Jesus will return in glory and with authority to judge all people.

PROPER RELATIONSHIPS. Verse 9 may seem a bit out of place, but our relationships relate to our need for endurance. As we wait for Jesus' arrival and endure difficulties, we need to have strong relationships with fellow believers. We shouldn't waste our time complaining about one another. Instead, our focus must be on living well in light of Jesus' impending arrival.

Instead of complaining about other believers, what should the characteristics of strong Christian friendship be?

This week how could you encourage endurance and patience in the other members of your Bible-study group?

James reminds us that pursuing holiness is a personal matter, but it isn't a private journey. Because we're related to one another in the body of Christ, we need one another. Our endurance isn't accomplished in a relational vacuum. It's lived out with all people of faith. It's critical that we refuse to complain but "watch out for one another to provoke love and good works" (Heb. 10:24).

LIKE THE PROPHETS AND JOB. James drew other great examples of endurance from the Old Testament. God called most of the prophets to deliver difficult messages to rebellious people in grueling periods of time. When we read the books of prophecy in the Old Testament, we find all sorts of stories that show us what endurance looks like. Jeremiah, the weeping prophet, remained steadfast in his ministry while the Israelites rebelled for decades. The Lord assigned Hosea to marry an unfaithful woman and then buy her back when she ran away. But they endured because they knew God's mercy is trustworthy and His judgment is certain.

The story of Job's enduring faith pierces our hearts. In the face of losing everything dear to him, including his children, Job refused to turn from a holy life. He endured, not because he wanted to regain what he lost but because he knew God is just and can be trusted.

James's examples challenge us to pursue holiness as we anticipate the end of time. We continue to join God's good purpose for the world and to grow in Christlikeness as we prepare for the time when we see Jesus face-to-face.

How should the trustworthy character of God change the way you view difficulties in life?

How does knowing that God will bring all things to completion in the end increase your willingness to endure trials and temptations?

Obedience in Real Time

"I'll clean up my room today." "The project will be done by the end of the week." "We're going to pay those bills immediately."

I think I've heard—and said—all these promises to be obedient. Plus a lot more. We all make promises. Some are kept, some are forgotten, and some are intentionally discarded. We all have responsibilities, but not everyone fulfills them. As we pursue a life of holiness, we must recognize the vital role of obedience in our walk with God.

Jesus, our example, was always obedient to the will of His Father. Look at a few of the statements he made about obedience:

> My food is to do the will of him who sent me and to finish his work.
> **John 4:34**

> I do as the Father commanded me.
> **John 14:31**

> If you keep my commands you will remain in my love, just as I have kept my Father's commands and remain in his love.
> **John 15:10**

This week we'll consider the idea of obedience in our everyday walk with Jesus. Obedience isn't just planning for a future date. Obedience is for this very moment, even as you read these lessons. While you're studying, if you discover that you've left undone a directive from the Lord, then set the book down and go do it. If your life is to be set apart for the purposes of God, it must be set apart immediately, consistently, and joyfully.

Start

....

Welcome everyone to session 2 of *Pursuing Holiness*. Use the following content to begin your group session together.

God calls us to be holy because He's holy (see Lev. 11:44). But what does the word *holy* mean? What does God expect us to do? To be?

> **How have you heard other people describe the concept of holiness?**

> **What role do you think morality plays in the concept of holiness? What else is part of it?**

Holiness is more than a moral code, although it includes that. God prescribed the law in the Old Testament and provided principles for holiness in the New Testament. When God gives us commands, it's reasonable to understand that we're supposed to follow them. We should be obedient.

After all, Jesus is our King. When we were saved, we placed ourselves under His authority. We put our faith in Jesus because we decided to follow Him in faith. Living the life of a disciple means learning from God's Word, heeding the conviction of God's Spirit, and submitting to the lordship of God's Son. All of this adds up to obedience.

> **What feelings do you have when you hear the word *obedience?***

God's call to holiness is a call to a imitate Jesus. It requires laying down certain attitudes and actions while taking up new ones. We move from a life defined by our own decisions and live in a way that's directed by God.

Pray that God will open your hearts and minds before you watch video session 2.

Watch

Use the space below to follow along and take notes as you watch video session 2.

We need to be able to do everything that God has requested of us
in real time.

Obedience starts with hearing and continues in our actions.

Holiness cannot be quarantined to a classroom setting.

Learning is of no real value if practice does not accompany it.

Faith and works are companions.

Old Testament examples remind us that faith has always been the gateway
to a relationship with God.

Our obedience is an outworking of our faith; it doesn't replace it.

Discuss

Use the following statements and questions to discuss the video.

The pursuit of holiness isn't just a mental pursuit the way a philosopher pursues an idea. Pursuing holiness happens in real time. Just as athletes practice for plays they'll execute in a game, we need to be ready to practice our faith in the real circumstances of life.

What's the danger of making holiness just a mental exercise?

Read aloud James 1:22-27.

What would make the biggest difference in helping you move from hearing the truth to acting on the truth?

Too often discipleship has been quarantined to a classroom setting. We can't treat the truth of God's Word like something to be dissected in a laboratory and left there while we reenter the world. There's no value to learning if we don't live according to what we've learned.

What's the danger of spending time learning the Word without any intention of obeying it?

God wants our faith to connect us with holy living, and that includes caring for people in need. Though some believers reject the word *religion,* James 1:27 gives us a definition of true religion that pleases God. It's a lifestyle of ministry, not merely a pursuit of knowledge. James used ministering to widows and orphans to represent ways to put our faith into practice.

What are some modern examples of exercising the type of faith that James 1:27 commends?

Pursuing holiness is more than just a mental exercise of acquiring theological knowledge. We take what we learn and experience in our study of God's Word and transfer it to active obedience in our lives.

Read aloud James 2:14-19.

Compare your own faith to the demonic faith that James described (see v. 19). How does that statement challenge you?

Pursuing holiness means our faith and our works are companions rather than competitors. Demons know that God is true in what He says and that they should obey Him. Yet they don't. When we fail to obey God's Word, we put ourselves in the same position as spiritual beings who oppose God's kingdom.

What's a biblical lesson that's often taught but seems to be difficult for many believers to obey? What makes obedience difficult?

Each circumstance of life is an opportunity to exercise what you've learned from God's Word. Just like an athlete who trains for a competition, this is your moment. The truth you've learned should shape the life you lead.

Read aloud James 2:20-26.

How do the characters of Abraham and Rahab differ? What was the common characteristic they shared?

Our works don't replace our faith. Instead, works respond to and display our faith. Abraham and Rahab were totally different types of people. They had different lives and were used by God in different ways. But what they had in common mattered: their faith, exercised in real time.

Conclude the group session with the prayer activity on the following page.

35

Pray

Conclude the group session by praying for yourself and group members in specific ways. Here are some prayer priorities to focus on before the next group session.

- Love for Christ that exceeds the joy you find in anything else

- Obedience to God in the face of temptations

- Unity in the church, centered on God's mission to take the gospel to the lost

- Joy in your life and in the lives of the members of your Bible-study group as you pursue holiness

- Faithfulness to Bible study and to a consistent prayer life that will draw you closer to God

Prayer Requests

Encourage members to complete "This Week's Plan" before the next group session.

This Week's Plan

Work with your group leader each week to create a plan for personal study, worship, and application between group sessions. Select from the following optional activities to match your personal preferences and available time.

Worship

[ ] Read your Bible. Complete the reading plan on page 38.

[ ] Spend time with God by engaging with the devotional experience on page 39.

[ ] Pray daily for the church and for group members.

Personal Study

[ ] Read and interact with "Holiness in Words and Actions" on page 40.

[ ] Read and interact with "Practicing Our Salvation" on page 44.

Application

[ ] Commit to a ministry in your church through which you can passionately serve others.

[ ] Memorize James 2:23: "The Scripture was fulfilled that says, Abraham believed God, and it was credited to him as righteousness, and he was called God's friend."

[ ] Add to your journal by recording an account of a time when another Christian positively influenced you by displaying his or her faith through actions.

[ ] Seek out a non-Christian friend with whom you can deepen your friendship through kind ministry in his or her life.

Did you miss the group session?
Video sessions available for purchase at lifeway.com/pursuingholiness

37

Read

Read the following Scripture passages this week. Use the acronym HEAR and the space provided to record your thoughts or action steps.

Day 1: John 15:12-17

Day 2: Matthew 5:13-17

Day 3: Psalm 1

Day 4: 1 John 4:7–5:4

Day 5: Proverbs 3:27-34

Day 6: Matthew 7:13-23

Day 7: Colossians 3:12-17

Reflect

PURSUED BY CHRIST

There's an old saying: Don't put the cart before the horse. In pursuing holiness, we must be careful to put things in their proper spiritual order.

Our pursuit of holiness is a result of having been pursued by Christ. It's a critical idea for us to catch in order to grow as a Christian. The work of Christ in us creates our desire and abilities to pursue holiness. Not the other way around:

> You are saved by grace through faith, and this is not from yourselves; it is God's gift—not from works, so that no one can boast. For we are his workmanship, created in Christ Jesus for good works, which God prepared ahead of time for us to do.
> **Ephesians 2:8-10**

We're saved by God's grace that was poured out on us through the work of Christ. When Jesus saved and purified us, He included plans for us to do good works that reflect His kingdom.

In fact, God planned these good works before our salvation. However, we can't pursue them until we've been captured by Jesus. As we seek maturity in Christ, we must do so in response to Jesus' grace, not in an effort to earn His approval.

A life of pursuing holiness begins with responding to what we've inherited from Christ. First we pursue Him; then we pursue a life that reflects His holiness by extension.

Personal Study 1

HOLINESS IN WORDS AND ACTIONS

Holiness must be pursued with our whole lives. The very nature of holiness demands that we wholly give our lives to God's purposes, refusing to hold back any portion of ourselves. Accordingly, we follow Jesus' answer to what was the most important command of the law:

> Jesus answered, "The most important is Listen, O Israel! The Lord our God, the Lord is one. Love the Lord your God with all your heart, with all your soul, with all your mind, and with all your strength."
> **Mark 12:29-30**

Create a chart that lists the four elements of the human life that Jesus identified. List three ways you can actively commit each element to Jesus during the next month.

From Our Ears to Our Hearts to Our Hands

Hearing the Bible is easy today because we have ready access to God's Word. We have multiple copies of the Bible in our homes. Dozens of Bible-reading apps are available. Innumerable podcasts exist for listening to preaching and Bible teaching.

Read James 1:19-25. What warning does this passage give us?

How can you guard against the problem of hearing but not acting according to the Scriptures?

This passage gives us an incredible promise. The person who takes God's directions seriously about who we are and how we should live "will be blessed in what he does" (v. 25). An athlete practices the same play over and over again to gain the muscle memory needed to act in real time. In the same way, we must hear God's Word again and again and look for ways we should obey in order to live holy lives in real time.

Why Our Words Matter

James then gave two specific directives for being obedient to Christ in our words and our actions. First he wrote:

> If anyone thinks he is religious without controlling his tongue,
> his religion is useless and he deceives himself.
> **James 1:26**

What's the connection between the teaching in verses 19-25 and the warning about controlling our speech that follows in verse 26?

In what circumstances do you have the most difficulty controlling your tongue?

Circle the issues that are difficult temptations for you.

Sarcasm	Insulting others	Cursing
Gossip	Angry answers	Backbiting
Dirty jokes (hearing and/or telling)		

We tend to excuse disobedience with our words. Little white lies, gossip, and hurtful criticism are excused as being lesser matters. Yet on numerous occasions Jesus taught about the power of our words. But it's not just a matter of the impact our words have on others. He also taught that the way we speak indicates something significant about our character.

The Pharisees asked Jesus why His followers didn't wash their hands before eating. Jesus responded by teaching what's really clean about a person (see Matt. 15:1-20). Notice what He said about our words:

> Summoning the crowd, he told them, "Listen and understand:
> It's not what goes into the mouth that defiles a person, but what
> comes out of the mouth—this defiles a person. What comes out
> of the mouth comes from the heart, and this defiles a person."
> **Matthew 15:10,18**

Our lives should be defined in every way by the power of the gospel. It's God's work in us that allows us to pursue holiness. So the way we speak should be characterized by the influence that has changed us. Our words should follow Jesus' work in us. Pursuing holiness often starts with obeying Jesus in what we say to others each day.

> Read Matthew 15:1-20. List Jesus' descriptions of ways our speech
> should sound. Then pray, asking God to help you change your
> words so that they give evidence of the gospel, encourage other
> people, and honor Him.

Why Our Actions Matter

After emphasizing our words, James then addressed our ministry to others. After all, our words and our actions are related. He wrote:

Pure and undefiled religion before God the Father is
this: to look after orphans and widows in their distress
and to keep oneself unstained from the world.
James 1:27

Why did James connect the ideas of caring for people in need and keeping ourselves morally pure?

This verse contains both offensive and defensive commands for pursuing a holy life (which is what James meant when he wrote "pure and undefiled religion"). We're to go forward in caring for the needy. Christians were supposed to bring relief to the lives of the poor. Why? Because this is what Jesus did. He intervened in the lives of those who were needy.

Defensively, believers are to separate ourselves from the sins of the world. Every day and every circumstance presents temptations for us. Christ's people should not only avoid the world's influence but also despise it. Christians are the proverbial fish swimming against the current. Holiness must be lived out in real time. We commit our lives to holiness as an ultimate goal for the future, but pursuing it requires commitment in the here and now.

List the names of three people in your immediate circle of friends who are in need, along with actions you can take to help them.

Pray about the stains of the world that are most attractive to you. If there's active sin in your life, ask God to forgive you and to help you resist the world's influence.

Personal Study 2

PRACTICING OUR SALVATION

"Put up or shut up." "Put your money where you mouth is." "Paint or get off the ladder." These sayings essentially challenge people to live up to what they claim to believe. Likewise, when we claim to be Christ followers, our faith should be obvious to everyone. James 2 encourages us to show our faith through good works.

> **Read James 2:14-26. As you read, record key phrases that help you understand the passage.**

In verses 14-16 James posed rhetorical questions to demonstrate that true faith in Christ will result in living out our relationship with Him. As we've previously learned, our good works don't earn salvation, but they're a response to it. We're on a pursuit of holiness in this life because through Jesus Christ we've been granted righteous standing before God for eternity.

Working on Behalf of Others

A significant way to reflect God's holiness in our lives is to care for others as Jesus did. After James asks us to reflect on the nature of the outward evidence of our inward faith, he offers a real-time opportunity.

First-century believers experienced persecution by their society and rejection by their families. Thus, many Christians commonly needed basic necessities. James used this real-life problem to reveal our eternal life change that comes by faith. If we've truly been changed by Christ, we'll seek to imitate His desire to aid others.

James bluntly stated that if you don't help with such obvious needs, you must not have true faith in Christ. The implication is that real faith seeks to bring about real change on behalf of others. Offering cute clichés doesn't do that. We're called to move past words to compassionate deeds.

> Think about the people in your closest relationships. What are their real needs? List their names and possible ways you can minister to them.

More than Believing an Idea

Faith isn't an intellectual belief in the right set of ideas. True faith in Christ means full surrender to Christ.

> Read James 2:18-19 and Acts 19:13-17. How would you describe the belief these evil spirits have in Jesus?

> How should our belief differ from theirs?

The demons who rebelled against God still mentally know He's the one true God. They recognize that He has ultimate authority. I suspect they even know their demise is eventually arriving. Yet they still rebel.

A believer's rebellion doesn't look like that of a demon. But James was using hyperbole. He was exaggerating to warn believers not to hold their faith only as a mental exercise rather than a working reality. Demons believe in God, but their belief isn't enough to save them. True belief changes the way we live. It's ridiculous for a Christian to profess in Jesus and then refuse to minister in His name.

> **Identify the most recent opportunity you've had to minister to another person, but you failed to do it. Take a few minutes to confess it and seek God's transformative grace to reorient your heart to ministry.**

Righteous Living from Utter Faith

We turn our attention from demons to an oddly paired couple of Old Testament characters: Abraham and Rahab. One was the father of the Israelite nation, and the other was a redeemed prostitute.

> **Read James 2:21-26. Underline the phrases that show how Abraham and Rahab gained right standing before God.**

James 2:23 quotes from Genesis 15:6 to reinforce our understanding that salvation comes by faith. Abraham's faith in God's work was the means by which righteousness was credited to his account. Like all of us, Abraham had sin on the ledger that demanded a payment. God covered that debt when Abraham placed his faith in God's atoning work. Whether someone lived before or after Christ, exercising faith is the only action required to receive God's righteousness.

Read the story of Rahab in Joshua 2. What leap of faith did Rahab take?

Rahab the prostitute acted in faith by helping the Hebrew spies when they scouted the promised land. She hid them when others hunted them because she was seeking rescue by the one true God of the Israelites. Both Abraham and Rahab had faith that was demonstrated by their actions.

What hope do you find in the fact that God offered salvation to both the good guy, Abraham, and the bad girl, Rahab? How does this challenge the way you think about faith?

What do their actions from faith teach you about doing good works in response to God's work in your life?

James presses us to pursue a life of obedience that reflects our salvation. As believers, we've inherited eternal life and received the Holy Spirit's presence. Our pursuit of holiness doesn't take place in a vacuum. It happens in a personal relationship with the God who saves, sanctifies, and prepares you for eternity in His presence.

Take time to pray about the following.
• The goodness of God's character that works in you
• Sins you've committed that you should repent of
• Areas in which God is calling you to deeper obedience
• Good works you can pursue in God's grace to display His salvation to others

Relationships
of Grace

Week 3

In downtown Nashville there's a large, two-lane traffic circle where three streets converge. I frequently drove through it while living there. The purpose of a traffic circle is to allow cars to move quickly through the intersection, thereby easing traffic. Its effectiveness depends on everyone's ability to yield properly. Therein lies the problem. Yielding.

On more than one occasion I saw the results of failing to understand this simple principle. It was usually a minor fender bender. But it was always a headache and probably involved at least a small degree of anger. A few seconds of aggressive driving resulted in police reports, the intervention of insurance agencies, and trips to the auto-repair shop. All because someone didn't want to yield or didn't know how to yield.

A pursuit of holiness isn't done in a relational vacuum. Rather, it's something believers do together, and it's observed by the lost people around us. Learning to yield our desires and preferences to the needs of others is a vital part of this pursuit, not only for our own spiritual growth but also for the benefit of unbelievers.

As in all matters of holiness, Jesus is our great example. He said:

> The Son of Man did not come to be served, but
> to serve, and to give his life as a ransom for many.
> **Matthew 20:28**

Seeking to live like Jesus—holy and set apart for God's purposes—will require us to live a yielded life in relationships of grace.

Start

Welcome everyone to session 3 of *Pursuing Holiness*. Use the following content to begin your group session together.

As a Christian, you have a deeply personal confession of faith in Jesus, but it's not a private confession. A relationship with Jesus reveals itself in every aspect of life. Because we've received His grace, we should willingly pass it on to others.

Relationships aren't always easy. Even under the best circumstances and even among believers, our egos can get in the way of truly caring for one another. We can become self-centered, expecting everyone to agree with just how amazing we think we are. It's in these moments that we need to receive grace—in large measure.

Describe a time when another Christian showed grace to you.

Experiencing grace from other Christians should challenge us to show it to others. But more than what our fellow believers do for us, it's what Christ has done that makes the greatest difference in our relationships. Jesus' work on our behalf to reconcile us to Himself has a profound effect on the way we relate to both believers and unbelievers.

How should your friendships be shaped by your salvation?

What type of people do you find most difficult to relate to?

Holiness as a way of life calls us to relate to people with a new mindset. We don't gauge the worth of people by their outward appearance or by what they can do for us. Instead, Christians have the opportunity to see others as God sees them: people who need His grace.

Pray that God will open your hearts and minds before you watch video session 3.

Watch

Use the space below to follow along and take notes as you watch video session 3.

The pursuit of holiness never occurs in a relational vacuum.

Grace for others is always a priority. You need to see people like Jesus saw you.

From the silly to the incredibly serious, whenever we look at another person, we need to make sure that we're seeing them as Jesus sees them.

We were covered by grace, and so that should be the lens that we use with other people.

Favoritism undermines the worth of people who need the grace that Christ so easily offers to us.

Holiness in your relationship means that you are driven by the fact that God has placed His image within that other person.

Our current relationships are not temporary issues, but they have eternal consequences.

Holiness is setting aside your will in favor of God's will that has to work in real time with real people in the world.

Discuss

Use the following statements and questions to discuss the video.

Relationships are the most common and the most difficult part of life. The people who surround us aren't just background set pieces. They're the people around whom we must live out our faith and live in holiness.

What types of people are the most difficult to be around and express your faith in Jesus?

Read aloud James 2:1-4.

What should be a church's normal reaction to someone who seems out of place in a worship service?

The illustration James offered regularly happens in our church services and ministries. People from various economic or cultural backgrounds attend, and we must respond to them. Our pursuit of holiness, rather than the person's condition in life, should drive our reaction. Holiness in our treatment of others means seeing people the way Jesus sees them.

How can a church actively work to eliminate favoritism in its relationships?

Read aloud James 2:5-7.

Why do we surrender to the temptation of favoring the powerful of the world instead of valuing the poor?

God often works in ways that seem counter to our thinking. We normally seek to get influence with people who can give us more influence. It would seem natural to use power to get more power. But God prefers something different. He wants us to trust in His power rather than the power of people in the world. A life of holiness means we trust that God's ways are right rather than aligning ourselves with worldly influence.

Read aloud James 2:8-11.

What does it mean to love someone else "as yourself" (v. 8)?

We forcibly protect our own lives. We can call it instinct, reflex, or drive. No matter what we call it, we naturally work to care for ourselves. Consider how it would radically change our lives if we lived as passionately for the good of other people.

How would living by God's will and ways display holiness in our relationships with others?

Read aloud James 2:12-13.

When are you most likely to actively judge other people?

What practical steps can you take to change from a perspective of judgment to a perspective of mercy?

Every relationship you have is with a person who will live for eternity in heaven or hell. Our pursuit of holiness involves all of those people. To live according to God's will means that we want what God wants for them. The Bible tells the story of God's desire to redeem people. Our pursuit of holiness should encourage others to understand God's greatest desire for them.

Conclude the group session with the prayer activity on the following page.

Pray

Conclude the group session by praying for yourself and group members in specific ways. Here are some prayer priorities to focus on before the next group session.

- Love for Christ that exceeds the joy you find in anything else

- Godly strength to resist temptations of favoritism

- Direction from the Holy Spirit about relationships you have with difficult people

- For the church to be filled with the love of Christ so that the mission of Christ will be the priority

- Faithfulness to Bible study and to a consistent prayer life that will draw you closer to God

Prayer Requests

Encourage members to complete "This Week's Plan" before the next group session.

This Week's Plan

Work with your group leader each week to create a plan for personal study, worship, and application between group sessions. Select from the following optional activities to match your personal preferences and available time.

Worship

[ ] Read your Bible. Complete the reading plan on page 56.

[ ] Spend time with God by engaging with the devotional experience on page 57.

[ ] Pray daily for the church and for group members.

Personal Study

[ ] Read and interact with "No More Favorites" on page 58.

[ ] Read and interact with "The Royal Law" on page 62.

Application

[ ] Identify a person with whom you should seek a deeper friendship.

[ ] Memorize James 2:1: "Do not show favoritism as you hold on to the faith in our glorious Lord Jesus Christ."

[ ] Journal about an occasion when another Christian reached out to you and ministered to you when you were having a difficult time.

[ ] List five people with whom you wish to share the gospel during the next few months.

Did you miss the group session?
Video sessions available for purchase at lifeway.com/pursuingholiness

55

Read

Read the following Scripture passages this week. Use the acronym HEAR and the space provided to record your thoughts or action steps.

Day 1: John 15:9-17

Day 2: Hebrews 10:24-25

Day 3: Ephesians 4:1-6

Day 4: Luke 6:27-36

Day 5: Acts 2:42-47

Day 6: Ephesians 4:25-31

Day 7: Colossians 3:12-17

Reflect

PURE LOVE

By their very nature, relationships require attention. The question we must ask is whether we're giving attention or demanding attention. Grace and holiness call us to be people who give not only attention to one another but also honor along with it. When we choose to focus on another person's needs, celebrations, and worth, we're living differently from the world's standards. Holiness that shows itself in grace-filled living makes believers stand out.

Consider Paul's teaching in Romans 12:9-21, one of the greatest passages on relationships in Scripture. But the only way to truly apply this passage is first to absorb the truths of Romans 1:1–12:8. The first three quarters of the book introduces us to the holiness of God, the horror of unrepentant sin, and the way Jesus changes the hearts of believers. With that background we're ready to apply teachings like these in Romans 12:

> Let love be without hypocrisy. … Outdo one another in showing honor. … Share with the saints in their needs; pursue hospitality. Bless those who persecute you. … Rejoice with those who rejoice.… Live in harmony with one another… Do not be conquered by evil, but conquer evil with good.
> **Romans 12:9-21**

The gospel described in Romans 1–11 changes us so that we can live as gospel people in the ways described in Romans 12–16. That's the way we pursue holiness. It's not a solo activity. God's holiness was put on display when He pursued a relationship with us. Now we can put His holiness on display in us as we pursue relationships with others. As we've been shown grace, we're called to show it to others.

Personal Study 1

NO MORE FAVORITES

I have two sons, Andrew and Chris. With an age difference of just twenty-two months, they're both young men now. They've always had a good relationship and had very few scuffles when they were young. They look alike, have similar mannerisms, and share the same sense of humor. But they have their differences.

As their parents, Angie and I have worked (hard!) not to play favorites with our boys. In their high-school and college years, they developed very distinct plans for the future and different interests. So we seek to value each of them for the individuals they've become.

But you know what's sometimes hard? Sometimes I like what one of them likes more than what the other one likes. Every now and then Andrew tells a story I think is hilarious, but Chris doesn't. Or Chris wants to watch a football game I want to watch, but Andrew is disinterested. In these moments I must remember that "love is kind" (1 Cor. 13:4).

> **When have you had to choose between activities with two people? How did you resolve the situation without playing favorites?**

> **If conflict resulted, what did you do to make amends?**

Giving Up Your Seat

In general, our culture is obsessed with exhibiting strength, posturing for position, and getting as much fame as possible. We like to be noticed, and we like to notice other people. Think about how many reality shows focus on people who've become famous for becoming famous. They didn't invent a world-changing medical device or discover the answer to one of life's great mysteries. Instead, they're beautiful, funny, audacious, fearless, or entertaining, so we watch them.

Would you watch a reality show or follow someone on social media who was weak, powerless, and needy? Why or why not?

Read James 2:1-4:

My brothers and sisters, do not show favoritism as you hold on to the faith in our glorious Lord Jesus Christ. For if someone comes into your meeting wearing a gold ring and dressed in fine clothes, and a poor person dressed in filthy clothes also comes in, if you look with favor on the one wearing the fine clothes and say, "Sit here in a good place," and yet you say to the poor person, "Stand over there," or "Sit here on the floor by my footstool," haven't you made distinctions among yourselves and become judges with evil thoughts?
James 2:1-4

In verse 1 James connected pursuing our faith with being equally kind to everyone. Holiness isn't something we do alone. Maturing in Christ means being careful to consider one another.

Honoring others matters not only in our personal relationships but also in the way we live as a congregation. Even the way we worship reveals whether we're pursuing holiness or being self-serving.

Have you ever avoided sitting with someone in a worship service because of his or her outward appearance? How did the Lord work in you after your decision?

What's revealed about a church that shows favoritism toward the financially rich?

When Christians show preferential treatment, it reveals that we've allowed evil intentions to rule our lives. We want to be around the rich and famous who can help us. We're looking for their presence to bolster our own lives. In contrast, Jesus' way is to come alongside the person in filthy clothing and an empty bank account. Showing grace for everyone matters in the kingdom of God.

Choosing the Weak

James also pointed out that God chooses poor people to be heirs of His kingdom. Our decision to choose the weak is both a mirror of God's character and a wise decision in pursuing holiness.

Read James 2:5-7. Underline the actions of the poor and the rich.

Listen, my dear brothers and sisters: Didn't God choose the poor in this world to be rich in faith and heirs of the kingdom that he has promised to those who love him? Yet you have dishonored the poor. Don't the rich oppress you and drag you into court? Don't they blaspheme the good name that was invoked over you?
James 2:5-7

How can a lower position in society encourage a person to have deeper faith in God?

In I Corinthians 1:26-31 the apostle Paul was helping a church in a large metropolitan city better understand how God works among believers. To people who lived where money talked and power screamed, Paul said:

> God has chosen what is foolish in the world to shame the wise, and
> God has chosen what is weak in the world to shame the strong. God
> has chosen what is insignificant and despised in the world—what is
> viewed as nothing—to bring to nothing what is viewed as something.
> **1 Corinthians 1:27-28**

It seems an odd choice. Why would anyone, including God, choose to relate to and work among people who are weak? Football teams recruit the best athletes. Companies hire the best candidates. Why? Because we want success. But God goes against the grain for a good reason. Paul continued:

> … so that no one may boast in his presence. It is from him that you
> are in Christ Jesus, who became wisdom from God for us—our
> righteousness, sanctification, and redemption, in order that,
> as it is written: Let the one who boasts, boast in the Lord.
> **1 Corinthians 1:29-31**

Showing favoritism to people who have worldly power runs counter to the ways of God. Those are the people who oppress us. The way of holiness is to choose weakness as the vessel through which God's great work in us and for us can be displayed.

When have you been guilty of showing favoritism? What adjustments do you need to make in order to serve people of all backgrounds?

Personal Study 2

THE ROYAL LAW

Sin is far too easily dismissed. "It wasn't a big deal." "No one got hurt." "It wasn't a major curse word." "Everyone is watching that show, doing that thing, laughing at those jokes, and saying the same things." We offer a long list of excuses and explanations as to why our sins haven't been so bad. But we forget that breaking any law makes us a lawbreaker.

When you were a kid, how did you try to get out of being punished?

What are the most common ways you've heard people excuse themselves from guilt over sin?

The Command of Love

As we're discovering, holiness is more than just making the right moral decision when faced with temptation. It's a matter of living out Christ's character that resides in us. It's a way of life.

In what way are you being most challenged to live out holiness today?

In James 2:8-11 we discover that setting our lives apart for Christ moves beyond moral choices. It extends even further than not showing favoritism:

If you fulfill the royal law prescribed in the Scripture, Love your neighbor as yourself, you are doing well. If, however, you show favoritism, you commit sin and are convicted by the law as transgressors. For whoever keeps the entire law, and yet stumbles at one point, is guilty of breaking it all. For he who said, Do not commit adultery, also said, Do not murder. So if you do not commit adultery, but you murder, you are a lawbreaker.
James 2:8-11

Refusing to show favoritism is motivated by something deeper. It comes from a life fueled by love. This idea is so important that James referred to it as "the royal law prescribed in the Scripture" (v. 8). The law of love is royal because it's anchored in the very nature of God. First John 4:16 says:

> We have come to know and to believe the love that
> God has for us. God is love, and the one who remains
> in love remains in God, and God remains in him.
> **1 John 4:16**

In pursuing holiness, we're ultimately pursuing Christ's presence in our lives. John shows us that to have God's presence in our lives is to have His character of love in our hearts as the key witness of who He is.

The Condemnation of Whims

The opposite of living by the royal law of love is fulfilling the whims of our flesh. When we give in to lust, anger, or another sin, it's an act of selfishness by which we look for ways to satisfy and promote ourselves.

List some ways our culture reinforces the value of self-promotion. Circle the ways you're guilty of self-promotion.

Read John 3:30. In what ways do you find that the pull toward self-promotion decreases as your desire to live a life of holiness increases?

How has the tendency toward self-promotion changed even as you've worked through this Bible study?

The way of love leads us to show grace to people in need rather than discard them as dead weight. Giving grace in our relationships reflects our love relationship with Jesus. The choice to love, which is the opposite of the choice to sin, imitates Jesus, who was the Suffering Servant. When we sin by promoting our self-interests to the exclusion of others, we act in childish ways that refuse to serve.

Consider the underprivileged people in your church family. How can you begin serving someone this week?

How will your service be a witness for Jesus and His good news?

The Commendation of Mercy

Sin ought to be punished because it's rebellion against God's right to rule our hearts and guide our lives. As Christians, then, we have a great reason to rejoice. Because Jesus paid for our sin on the cross, we now live under grace, and we get to extend grace to other people. James wrote:

> Speak and act as those who are to be judged by the law
> of freedom. For judgment is without mercy to the one who
> has not shown mercy. Mercy triumphs over judgment.
> **James 2:12-13**

List words that describe what you think it will be like to stand before God after you die.

According to the previous passage, by what standard will Christians be judged?

Jesus' mercy will triumph over our judgment. Grace will win. The judgment we deserved was placed on Christ when He served as our sin offering on the cross. His righteousness enables us to live holy lives.

The bondage of ego, sin, and selfishness convinces us to hold people down and make them serve us. It tells us to hang out with the beautiful people, sit at the cool kids' table, and seek to be the sidekicks of people with power.

Christians are called to a new way of relating to people. All of our words and all of our actions are now guided by the law of freedom. We live like Jesus in our relationships. You see, before our salvation we were the poor people who stood at the back of the room or sat on the floor, unworthy of even a chair. But now God's mercy overrides the judgment we deserve. And now we can pass on that mercy to others.

Think of friends who need mercy, grace, and love. Record their names, along with the causes of their pain. Then identify one way you can seek to meet their needs.

"Mercy triumphs over judgment" (v. 13) is a beautiful sentence. It has an eternal impact that describes God's work in Christ for sinners. James used it to remind us that our pursuit of holiness means living in relationships with people who need our love instead of our judgment. Let mercy win this week.

Putting Holiness into Practice

"If you don't have anything nice to say, then say nothing at all." It's a cliché we teach our kids to help them control what they say. The only problem is that we're normally left with nothing to say.

So far in this Bible study, we've given a lot of emphasis to displaying holiness in our actions. Now we're going to make sure our words are in line with our pursuit of a life that reflects a Christlike character.

James 3 challenges us to recognize the power in our words. Our words have the power to harm, but they also have the power to reveal divine wisdom and to display a person's integrity. We can use our words as instruments for holiness.

The tongue is perhaps the most powerful muscle in the body. Proverbs 18:21 teaches:

> Death and life are in the power of the tongue,
> and those who love it will eat its fruit.
> **Proverbs 18:21**

When we open our mouths to comment on another person's behavior, criticize an idea, propose a change, or declare a theological idea, we're wielding great power. That's why our parents told us to speak only if we had something good to say.

The passages we'll consider this week will both remind and guide us to use the power of our words and actions carefully.

Start

"Sticks and stones may break my bones, but words will never hurt me" is just about the most misleading rhyme we ever teach to kids. We do it to convince them that they can disregard mean comments and that they're people of value, no matter what others say. But we all know that words have great power in our lives.

What's the greatest compliment you've ever received?

What's the oddest criticism that has come your way?

Just discussing these stories drives home the power Scripture ascribes to our words. Proverbs 15:4 says:

> The tongue that heals is a tree of life,
> but a devious tongue breaks the spirit.
> **Proverbs 15:4**

As Christians, we're called to set apart every aspect of our lives for the purposes of God. Our pursuit of holiness includes the use of our words.

In this session be willing to honestly evaluate the way you use your words. If you use too much biting sarcasm or gossip, seek to become "a tree of life" instead. In our pursuit of a life that reflects Jesus' transformation, let your words heal like His.

Pray that God will open your hearts and minds before you watch video session 4.

Watch

Use the space below to follow along and take notes as you watch video session 4.

As we pursue holiness, we have to choose some new defaults in our life so that we can put holiness into practice.

You need to test your tongue.

1. Is it sacred truth or sarcastic barbs?

2. Is it Bible or backbiting?

3. Is it gospel or gossip?

The wisdom you choose to use is based on the way you want to live your life.

You've got to choose. Are you going to be motivated by the things of the world, or are you going to be motivated by God's kingdom, covenant, and mission?

Holiness is designed to make you look like Jesus, and Jesus looked like a servant.

Discuss

Use the following statements and questions to discuss the video.

We all have habits that kick in with the normal paces of life.

What habits help you get through a tough day?

Read aloud James 3:1-8.

What are some common ways people stumble by using their words poorly?

This passage reminds us that being a teacher of the truth is often a difficult position to be in because we stumble in our use of words. We can use our tongues to do great things, but they also have the potential to do great harm.

What do the images of horses, boats, and fire contribute to your understanding of the power of the tongue?

Our words can be a blessing, but they can also get completely out of control. A powerful animal, a ship without a rudder, and a fire can all have destructive power. When tamed, these are great servants. But out of control, they make horrible masters. The same is true of our words. They can be used for great good or great evil.

Read aloud James 3:9-12.

What causes you to lose control and speak poorly to other people?

Jesus said our mouths speak only as an overflow of the heart (see Luke 6:45). When we pursue holiness, we're pursuing a life like the one Jesus lived. Such a life consistently blesses God and others. Therefore, our use of words is another reason for us to desire a deep, heartfelt devotion to Christ. Our words indicate where our affections are—on Jesus or on our selfish desires.

Read aloud James 3:13-16.

How do the worldly motivations of hoarding things, achieving more, and gaining a reputation contribute to an unholy life?

Our conduct—including our words—should reflect the heavenly wisdom we gain through holy living. James said in verse 13 that our works will be done in gentleness if we live according to God's wisdom. The opposite of a gentle, holy life is "earthly, unspiritual, demonic" (v. 15) living that comes from living for the world's motivations. Holiness isn't something that automatically happens to you. It's a life you must pursue by the power of the Holy Spirit. There are too many temptations that will trip you up otherwise.

Read aloud James 3:17-18.

What descriptor of holy living in verse 17 needs attention in your life?

Being aware of our strengths and weaknesses is a key element for putting holiness into practice. We won't always be clearheaded in knowing ways we need to mature. But that's why we have friends and a Bible-study group. We can guide one another to know how to grow in holiness.

How can you actively help and pray for group members to pursue holiness more effectively?

Conclude the group session with the prayer activity on the following page.

Pray

Conclude the group session by praying for yourself and group members in specific ways. Here are some prayer priorities to focus on before the next group session.

- Love for Christ that exceeds the joy you find in anything else

- Words that build up another person's faith this week

- Strength to resist the temptations to gossip, insult, and otherwise use your words sinfully

- For the church to be a place of encouragement for people who are suffering

- For wisdom to be displayed through your life as you talk about the gospel and God's Word with others

- Faithfulness to Bible study and to a consistent prayer life that will draw you closer to God

Prayer Requests

Encourage members to complete "This Week's Plan" before the next group session.

This Week's Plan

Work with your group leader each week to create a plan for personal study, worship, and application between group sessions. Select from the following optional activities to match your personal preferences and available time.

Worship

[ ] Read your Bible. Complete the reading plan on page 74.

[ ] Spend time with God by engaging with the devotional experience on page 75.

[ ] Pray daily for the church and for group members.

Personal Study

[ ] Read and interact with "Controlling the Tongue" on page 76.

[ ] Read and interact with "A Gently Powerful Life" on page 80.

Application

[ ] Identify a person in your life who's been a great encouragement to you. Take the time to let that person know how much he or she means to you.

[ ] Memorize James 3:18: "The fruit of righteousness is sown in peace by those who cultivate peace."

[ ] Journal about your personal need to be holy in using language. Ask God to strengthen you in areas where you've been tempted to sin with your words.

[ ] Seek out a friend who needs direction from the Bible. Share the gospel with a lost person or some biblical encouragement with a saved friend.

Did you miss the group session?
Video sessions available for purchase at lifeway.com/pursuingholiness

73

Read

Read the following Scripture passages this week. Use the acronym HEAR and the space provided to record your thoughts or action steps.

Day 1: Ephesians 4:25-32

Day 2: Proverbs 10:11-21

Day 3: 1 Peter 3:8-12

Day 4: Proverbs 15:1-7

Day 5: Colossians 4:2-6

Day 6: Matthew 15:1-11

Day 7: Psalm 96:2-4

Reflect

THE GREATEST USE OF YOUR WORDS

The theme of Psalm 119, the longest chapter in the Bible, is the power of God's Word. But near the end it focuses on our use of words:

> Let my cry reach you, LORD;
> give me understanding according to your word.
> Let my plea reach you;
> rescue me according to your promise.
> My lips pour out praise,
> for you teach me your statutes.
> My tongue sings about your promise,
> for all your commands are righteous.
> **Psalm 119:169-172**

CRY FOR UNDERSTANDING. We consistently face circumstances that require wisdom. We don't just need the facts; those come from simple observation. We need to cry out to God that He will use His Word to give us wisdom for everyday decisions.

PLEAD FOR RESCUE. This world can be brutal. When we feel the waves of despair overtaking us, we plead to God for His rescuing work. He takes delight in delivering His people.

PRAISE FOR LEARNING. We don't often connect praise and learning, but the psalmist did. We should praise God because He teaches us truth. He leads us in ways to live according to His Word. He deserves our adoration for walking with us in such a personal way.

SING FOR WORSHIP. God deserves our songs that focus on His character and His commands. We use the commodity of our words to focus attention on the God who's great, holy, and beautiful.

Personal Study 1

CONTROLLING THE TONGUE

An excuse unbelievers often give for not coming to church is that they prefer to be spiritual and not religious. Their excuse also shows up in the form of the statement "I don't like organized religion." But James emphasized that there's a form of religion we should embrace.

Talking the Walk

As Christians, we're public examples of personal faith in Christ. We need to continually test whether our words and our religion match:

> If anyone thinks he is religious without controlling his tongue,
> his religion is useless and he deceives himself.
> **James 1:26**

Why would James connect the ideas of controlling our tongues and caring for distressed people?

If we really want to learn how to control our tongues, a great step is to understand how our words are embedded in the rest of our lives. We're skilled at putting portions of our lives in different compartments. When we give our lives to Christ, He intends to change every part of us. He wants us to be useful for His kingdom purposes. Our words and our actions are more connected than ever before.

The warning of James 1:26 ought to set off an alarm in our hearts. We can sing beautifully in worship, serve well in the church, and be good neighbors, but if we let our mouths get out of control, our religious lives are inadequate.

Record three instances when you've been frustrated by circumstances or people, the way you were tempted to misuse your words, and a point of prayer for those moments.

Circumstance	Temptation	Prayer

Proverbs 15:4 reminds us that "a devious tongue breaks the spirit." The psalmist says our words can tear down another person. James tells us our poor use of words can not only break down another person but can also deceive us about what it means to live a holy life.

A Wild Ride or a Fruitful Life

When our two sons were kids, my wife and I took them to a number of theme parks, where they rode a lot of roller coasters. Like most kids, they were anxious at first but were then thrilled to jump back on the rides. We rode some of them so many times that I had the tracks memorized and knew what was around each turn. If only life could be that way.

Instead, we're thrown into a multitude of random issues on a daily basis. Not knowing which way the proverbial winds will blow, we have to be ready for any challenge. But perhaps one of the most significant challenges is internal rather than external.

Read James 3:1-12. Circle the images in verses 1-8 that most effectively help you understand the power of your words.

¹Not many should become teachers, my brothers, because you know that we will receive a stricter judgment. ²For we all stumble in many ways. If anyone does not stumble in what he says, he is mature, able also to control the whole body. ³Now if we put bits into the mouths of horses so that they obey us, we direct their whole bodies. ⁴And consider ships: Though very large and driven by fierce winds, they are guided by a very small rudder wherever the will of the pilot directs. ⁵So too, though the tongue is a small part of the body, it boasts great things. Consider how a small fire sets ablaze a large forest. ⁶And the tongue is a fire. The tongue, a world of unrighteousness, is placed among our members. It stains the whole body, sets the course of life on fire, and is itself set on fire by hell. ⁷Every kind of animal, bird, reptile, and fish is tamed and has been tamed by humankind, ⁸but no one can tame the tongue. It is a restless evil, full of deadly poison. ⁹With the tongue we bless our Lord and Father, and with it we curse people who are made in God's likeness. ¹⁰Blessing and cursing come out of the same mouth. My brothers and sisters, these things should not be this way. ¹¹Does a spring pour out sweet and bitter water from the same opening? ¹²Can a fig tree produce olives, my brothers and sisters, or a grapevine produce figs? Neither can a saltwater spring yield fresh water.
James 3:1-12

What emotions do you experience when you read the phrases you circled?

Although the church needs teachers, James asserted that not everyone should fill that role. One reason is that not all of us can control our words. James pressed this point home with a few word pictures.

1. Our mouths can be like a bit inserted into the mouth of a horse to control its movement. How often has your life been totally altered by your mouth? One overly sarcastic remark can ruin a conversation. On the other hand, one well-stated word of encouragement can deepen a friendship.

2. Our mouths can be like the rudder of a ship. Regardless of the power of the circumstances around us, our mouths can be the key to staying on course. We can confess our confidence in God, even in a storm, or we can scream in frustration with Him. The little rudder of our words can set us on very different courses.

3. The tongue is like fire. It has the power to warm us, cook food, and purge what isn't needed. Or it can be the most destructive force in nature.

4. Many animals can be tamed, but the human tongue seems to break loose on a regular basis.

5. Verse 8 says the tongue is "a restless evil, full of deadly poison." We're tempted to spill poison through our words about people we don't like or even about people we like. Our words should reflect the fruitful ministry of Jesus by blessing others. The way of holiness is to give grace rather than curses.

Pursuing holiness requires single-mindedness. Jesus came in a ministry of grace and truth (see John 1:14). As His followers, we're to speak the truth in love (see Eph. 4:15). Only the gospel's transformative power can help us bear good fruit through our words.

> **Take time to confess to the Lord any sins you've recently committed with your tongue. Be specific about any immature comments, gossip, profane jokes, or disrespectful statements you've made to God. Allow Him to convict you and lead you to repentance.**

Personal Study 2

A GENTLY POWERFUL LIFE

One reason I love the Book of James is that it connects various parts of the Christian life to the whole. We don't get off the hook by working on one dimension of our character while ignoring the other qualities. Instead, James challenges us to see how every part of life connects with the others.

The way to holiness requires that we see the interconnectivity of our character development. The Gospels present Jesus to us as the perfect man. His moral purity, of course, stemmed from His divinity. But He lived out His holy character in the same context of work, relationships, and world conditions that we experience. In the incarnation Jesus revealed His perfect character in His attitudes, intentions, actions, and words.

Recall from our previous study that James 3:1-12 focused on the power of the tongue—how our words can be products of holiness or evil. James then transitioned to the subject of living with godly wisdom:

> Who among you is wise and understanding? By his good conduct he should show that his works are done in the gentleness that comes from wisdom. But if you have bitter envy and selfish ambition in your heart, don't boast and deny the truth. Such wisdom does not come down from above but is earthly, unspiritual, demonic. For where there is envy and selfish ambition, there is disorder and every evil practice. But the wisdom from above is first pure, then peace-loving, gentle, compliant, full of mercy and good fruits, unwavering, without pretense. And the fruit of righteousness is sown in peace by those who cultivate peace.
> **James 3:13-18**

Among the godly characteristics listed in this passage, which ones are you currently experiencing the most in your life?

Which ones are you currently struggling to incorporate into your life?

What help could you seek from a Christian friend to encourage you toward holiness in these areas?

Two Types of Wisdom

Our Christian faith is lived out on a battleground, not a playground. We aren't just playing tag or waiting for a turn on the slide. Our choices aren't between one good thing and another good thing. In life we operate by divine, holy wisdom or demonic, worldly thinking. We don't have a middle ground to choose.

Here are some examples of truth claims that people make. Mark each one with either G for *godly wisdom* or W for *worldly thinking*.
___ Serving others
___ Being argumentative
___ Doing whatever it takes to get a promotion
___ Working hard for the good of a team
___ Yelling as loudly as the other person during a conflict
___ Embarrassing a family member for a good laugh
___ Taking extra time on a visit with a friend
___ Generously giving financially to someone in need
___ Using shame with your children to ensure obedience
___ Waiting for a person in need to beg before helping

The passage we read makes it clear that holiness produces fruit that's easily perceived in our actions. Verse 17 lists some of the results of reliance on holy wisdom as being "pure, then peace-loving, gentle, compliant, full of mercy and good fruits, unwavering, without pretense." We must learn how to pursue these holy qualities without inflating our egos. Believers who boast or show off because of their good actions essentially undermine any development of their character. Pursuing Christ, doing ministry, and being holy must be free of "selfish ambition" (v. 14) and "without pretense" (v. 17).

How does pride interrupt our pursuit of holiness?

Actions, Words, and Responses

Our words are extensions of our character. James 3:14 states:

> If you have bitter envy and selfish ambition
> in your heart, don't boast and deny the truth.
> **James 3:14**

If sin takes root in your life, your words will reflect what's in your heart. There's no escape. It's the squeeze principle. When life's pressures squeeze you, the truth of your character will come out.

What pressures are squeezing you or have recently squeezed you?

List your responses to the pressure. Be honest and indicate whether they reflect holiness or a sinful response.

We live an integrated life. Our words, our egos, and our actions constantly intersect. James 3:18 states, "The fruit of righteousness is sown in peace by those who cultivate peace." Pursuing holiness isn't chasing something elusive. We're not hunting and ambushing holiness to shove into our lives. We cultivate these characteristics of holiness in our lives.

What are you doing to cultivate holiness in your life? Circle the actions you're currently engaged in, underline the actions you periodically take, and draw a star beside the actions you want to begin in the near future.

___ Bible-reading plan   ___ Intercessory prayer
___ Attending worship services ___ Group Bible study
___ Offering encouragement   ___ Personal Bible study
___ Fasting   ___ Personal witnessing
___ Serving in a church ministry ___ Showing hospitality
___ Peacemaking between people in conflict

A life of holiness reveals integrity. Obviously, hypocrisy is the opposite of what we're pursuing. We want our passions, words, and actions to align with the character of Jesus. A final example is found in James 5:12:

> Above all, my brothers and sisters, do not swear, either by heaven or by earth or with any other oath. But let your "yes" mean "yes," and your "no" mean "no," so that you won't fall under judgment.
> **James 5:12**

Again, the instruction to live out our holiness is accompanied by a warning. Holiness is serious business. We must cultivate it with a passionate heart that seeks full alignment with the character of Christ.

The Way of Humility

I still remember the cover of a Bible study I did in my high-school years. It was during a discipleship weekend in which students gathered in groups according to age and gender in church members' homes from Friday afternoon until Sunday morning. We did intensive Bible study during the day, gathered for worship on Friday and Saturday nights, and stayed up most of the night playing games. This particular year the Bible-study booklet had a bright yellow cover and was titled "Meekness Is Not Geekness." I know. It was an awful title but obviously memorable.

I don't remember all the details about that study, but I remember the theme: rather than constantly acting like a normal teenager who's looking for recognition, get low and serve people. We all knew we needed the lesson, but it was hard to put into practice.

The world pushes us to push ourselves. Even as I've written this study, self-centered thoughts have tried to elevate themselves above the message of James. Elements like cover design, marketing plans, the right head shot for the author page, and suitable clothing for the video shoot passed through my mind. But the words of James are so much more meaningful than these details.

The way to holiness is the low way. Holiness doesn't aggrandize self. It can't have a big head but must have a big heart. To pursue holiness is to look like Jesus, and Jesus looked like a servant.

Start

Welcome everyone to session 5 of *Pursuing Holiness*. Use the following content to begin your group session together.

The world doesn't promote the virtue of humility. In general, businesses, sports, workplace relationships, and homeowner associations often function by competition. From kids running for elementary-school class president to candidates vying for the CEO position in a company, submitting to someone else isn't the way of this world.

But it's the way of holiness. Think how absurd humility must appear to the world. The way ahead is to bow low. The way forward is to give way to others.

What's your most recent memory of competing with someone else?

How did competition affect your relationship with that person?

In this session we'll look at James 4. This passage effortlessly moves back and forth between our relationship with God and our relationships with other people. Although they may seem to be completely different subjects, they aren't. The dual emphasis reveals that we always occupy third place in our relationships. God is our top priority, and everyone else comes second. As Christ followers pursuing holiness, we must learn to live in third place.

How does the world view the idea of humility?

The pursuit of holiness means the pursuit of glory for Another and the well-being of others. It's not that we refuse to care for ourselves. After all, Jesus said we're to love our neighbor as we love ourselves (see Matt. 22:39). Our task is to let the humility of Christ shape our holiness in such a way that we love God, other people, and ourselves in the proper order.

Pray that God will open your hearts and minds before you watch video session 5.

Watch

Use the space below to follow along and take notes as you watch video session 5.

Holiness is the pursuit of a life that is totally and unalterably set apart for the will and the ways of God.

Holiness demands the abandonment of selfish whims, wishes, and wants.

Jesus has changed our eternal trajectory, and now day by day He is sanctifying our lives and our hearts so that we will look more and more like Him.

Baal was the god of more.

Grace is the gift of God that you never earned.

The way of holiness means that you're living like Jesus, and Jesus comes as a servant, surrendering everything that would have benefited Him for the good of the people around Him.

Humility before God must translate into humble service for others.

Humility before God can be used by the King to benefit His kingdom and everybody else around you.

Discuss

We find it to be almost distressing when another person humbly tells us that he or she needs our help. We've grown accustomed to pride-filled people bulldozing their way forward in life. Taking the way of humility is counter to our human nature. That's precisely the reason humility is the way of holiness.

Read aloud James 4:1-3.

When you were a kid, what was the most common reason for arguments and fights with your friends?

Kids disagree when they don't get their way. Whether it's picking team members for kickball or choosing jobs in a group project, we want to get what we want. When that doesn't happen, tempers flare up into arguments and conflict. As believers, we must choose better motives (see v. 3) so that we can pursue God's will and God's ways for every circumstance.

What's an occasion when Jesus showed great humility?

Jesus committed His life to humble service. Even though He deserved to be served, He chose to serve. He actively lived under God's will so that other people could benefit from His work. Holiness demands that we abandon any selfish whims and wishes so that God can work through us.

In the Old Testament we read about people who worshiped the false god Baal. This deity supposedly blessed crops with fruitfulness, business with economic gain, and people with fertility. He was the god of more. But as Christians, we need to want more than the more that the world offers.

Read aloud James 4:4-10.

How will choosing to serve propel your pursuit of holiness?

Our pride will lead us to align with the worst evil. In contrast, humility can guide us to submit fully to God's work. It isn't difficult to see that one quality is filled with joy, while the other is filled with misery.

Read aloud James 4:11-12.

How does humbling ourselves before God relate to the way we treat other people?

A life of humility allows you to see people as God sees them, as people made in His image with inherent worth. A holy outlook is a Godlike outlook. We need to put on the lenses of the Kingdom.

Read aloud James 4:13-17.

How often do you think about the hereafter? How do those thoughts affect the way you make daily decisions?

Seeing life in view of eternity sharpens our focus on holy living by putting all of this life in the proper context. We realize that all decisions involve others and that all people will live for eternity in either heaven or hell. We need to allow God's plans for our lives to drive the decisions we make in every arena, from business to friendships.

Conclude the group session with the prayer activity on the following page.

Pray

Conclude the group session by praying for yourself and group members in specific ways. Here are some prayer priorities to focus on before the next group session.

- Love for Christ that exceeds the joy you find in anything else

- For humility to serve another person today who needs kindness

- Unity in the church so that humble service will characterize its reputation in the community

- Humility before God in seeking the power of the Holy Spirit to live a holy life

- Faithfulness to Bible study and to a consistent prayer life that will draw you closer to God

Prayer Requests

Encourage members to complete "This Week's Plan" before the next group session.

This Week's Plan

Work with your group leader each week to create a plan for personal study, worship, and application between group sessions. Select from the following optional activities to match your personal preferences and available time.

Worship

[ ] Read your Bible. Complete the reading plan on page 92.

[ ] Spend time with God by engaging with the devotional experience on page 93.

[ ] Pray daily for the church and for group members.

Personal Study

[ ] Read and interact with "Humble Holiness" on page 94.

[ ] Read and interact with "Active Humility" on page 98.

Application

[ ] This week find and minister to a lost person who needs encouragement and hope. Contact the person and set a time when you can meet.

[ ] Memorize James 4:7: "Submit to God. Resist the devil, and he will flee from you."

[ ] Journal about the humility of Jesus Christ. Record your thoughts about a portion of His life that exemplifies humility.

[ ] Identify an important decision you need to make and submit it to God in prayer. Commit to spending additional time in prayer about obeying God's direction.

Did you miss the group session?
Video sessions available for purchase at lifeway.com/pursuingholiness

91

Read

Read the following Scripture passages this week. Use the acronym HEAR and the space provided to record your thoughts or action steps.

Day 1: I Peter 5:6-11

Day 2: Zephaniah 2:1-3

Day 3: Colossians 3:12-17

Day 4: Psalm 25:8-15

Day 5: Hebrews 5:1-10

Day 6: Matthew 20:20-28

Day 7: Philippians 2:5-8

Reflect

TWO BOWLS OF WATER

At the end of Jesus' life, we find two bowls of water. The contrast between these simple vessels gives incredible insight into the way we should live.

At the last supper in John 13, the apostles had gathered in a room to eat the Passover meal. In this ancient Middle Eastern home they were seated on the floor, reclining and eating at a very short table. Thus, their feet extended out from the table. At the end of the meal, Jesus put a towel around His waist, got a bowl of water, and started washing the feet of His disciples.

He washed the feet of the ten men who would disappear into the night after he was arrested. He washed the feet of Simon Peter, who would deny knowing Jesus three times that night. He even washed the feet of the betrayer in their midst, Judas Iscariot. Through this act Jesus served His disciples to set an example for them—and for us.

A second bowl of water is mentioned in Matthew 27:21-24. Jesus had been dragged from one trial to another during the night following His arrest. The governor, Pilate, presented Jesus, along with the murdering insurrectionist Barabbas, for the crowd of Jews to decide who would escape crucifixion. The crowd demanded Jesus' execution. Pilate asked in verse 23, "Why? What has he done wrong?" But they wanted Jesus dead. Pilate took some water and washed his hands in a symbolic gesture, saying, "I am innocent of this man's blood" (v. 24).

Each day we must decide which bowl of water we'll take up. We can choose the bowl of Pilate and wash our hands of the whole mess of life, faithfulness, and other people's needs. The better way is to take up the bowl of Christ and serve, even though it sometimes means washing the feet of others who will abandon, deny, and even betray us.

Personal Study 1

HUMBLE HOLINESS

Humility isn't just an inner character trait. It starts there, but it must be expressed in all our interactions. When we treat humility exclusively as a spiritual posture toward God, we neglect opportunities He gives us to work out our salvation on earth (see Phil. 2:12-13). Humility encompasses the way we think about and live our lives here, not just in the hereafter.

List three people who embody humility. Identify ways they display humility.

What lessons can you learn from these people?

After teaching on the ways we use our words and connect with God's heavenly wisdom, James turned his attention to the humble interactions we need to have in life.

As you read James 4:1-12, draw a box around each instruction that's a struggle for you.

What is the source of wars and fights among you? Don't they come from your passions that wage war within you? You desire and do not have. You murder and covet and cannot obtain. You fight and wage war. You do not have because you do not ask. You ask and don't receive because you ask with wrong motives, so that you may spend it on your pleasures. You adulterous people! Don't you know that friendship with the world is hostility toward God? So whoever wants to be the friend of the world becomes the enemy of God.

Or do you think it's without reason that the Scripture
says: The spirit he made to dwell in us envies intensely?
But he gives greater grace. Therefore he says:

> God resists the proud,
>
> but gives grace to the humble.

Therefore, submit to God. Resist the devil, and he will flee from you. Draw near to God, and he will draw near to you. Cleanse your hands, sinners, and purify your hearts, you double-minded. Be miserable and mourn and weep. Let your laughter be turned to mourning and your joy to gloom. Humble yourselves before the Lord, and he will exalt you. Don't criticize one another, brothers and sisters. Anyone who defames or judges a fellow believer defames and judges the law. If you judge the law, you are not a doer of the law but a judge. There is one lawgiver and judge who is able to save and to destroy. But who are you to judge your neighbor?

James 4:1-12

Be Content with What You Have

James opened this chapter with a rhetorical question about the source of our wars and fights. On a global scale we wage war to gain land, control populations, and acquire what other countries possess. On a personal level we do the same. Envy and jealousy cause all of our fights and quarrels. We fight because we want more.

What was the last item you purchased because someone else had one? In retrospect would you have purchased this item again?

The discontented state of our hearts drives us to discount the needs of other people. When we can't be happy because someone else has something we don't have, humility doesn't characterize our lives. Humility consistently looks out for the needs of others and celebrates God's work in their lives. A humble life offers an image of Jesus for others to see.

This attitude must extend even to the way we pray. We look out for others, but we also humbly ask God to provide for our own needs. Sadly, James said we often pray poorly and ask with selfish motives (see v. 3).

> **Perhaps your prayer life needs some fine-tuning. List requests you're regularly making to God. Ask the Holy Spirit for wisdom to make the right requests with a spirit of humility.**

Submit and Resist

Humility won't arise from our own efforts. As in all of our Christian walk, it's a product of God's work in our lives. This is why James commands us to "submit to God" (v. 7). Service is the outcome when we allow God to fully direct every step. In the following verse we're reminded, "Draw near to God, and he will draw near to you" (v. 8). Because our hearts have a natural inclination toward pride, we need to dwell in a close relationship with Christ so that He can plant godly traits like humility in our hearts.

There's another side to this critical equation. James also commands us, "Resist the devil," along with the encouragement "and he will flee from you" (v. 7). We have a real adversary who never wants us to cultivate humility as a way of life. Satan's preference is that we continue to swell in pride in our own abilities and wallow in self-pity when someone else surpasses us. But when we develop resistance to him that's fueled by submission to our true Master, the enemy doesn't stand a chance of influencing us.

A price comes with our pursuit of holy, humble living. We must be cleansed, purify our hearts, and grieve over any sin in our lives (see vv. 8-9). This doesn't mean that God wants us to be miserable but that He wants us to be fully aware of the misery brought about by sin. Eternal life has been secured by the Holy Spirit's work and presence in our lives. But God also wants us to live free from the power of sin. By confessing and repenting of sin—agreeing with God and turning from sinful patterns—we can habitually live in holiness and grow in Christlike character.

> **Rewrite the commands of verses 7-10 in your own words. Then apply the commands to specific spiritual needs in your life.**

Be Humble in Your Relationships

We're really good at playing the role of judge. It's easier to find fault in others than in ourselves. But verses 11-12 clearly teach that only God is the rightful Judge over people. When we try to take God's place at the Judge's bench, we insult the work He does perfectly.

Humility refuses the opportunity to condemn another person. A set-apart life means believers are ministers of reconciliation (see 2 Cor. 5:18-19) rather than judges. This is why we must be sensitive to the people we meet. Lost people need to see in us a portrait of the God who desires to save. Hurting people need to see and hear the message of the Comforter who's always present. Fellow believers need encouragement to press on.

> **Take time to pray for lost people, hurting people, and fellow believers. Ask God how you can intercede for and serve them with humility.**

Personal Study 2

ACTIVE HUMILITY

A myth that must be dispelled is the idea that humility is the same as passivity. In a culture that values aggression, any mention of humility seems counterproductive. But humility isn't the desire to coast along in neutral while the world passes us by. Instead, it's a state of mind that seeks God's will so that we can actively follow it. Holiness is the desire to be in the middle of God's ongoing work.

What are the top three areas of your life in which you would like to know God's will?

Complete the following statements with raw honesty, using a scale of I to 5: I = strongly disagree, 2 = disagree, 3 = possible, 4 = agree, 5 = strongly agree.

___ In the past year I've obeyed God in most matters.

___ I'll answer God's call on my life, no matter where it takes me.

___ Currently, I have sin in my life that I find difficult to let go.

___ God can count on me to be faithful in sharing the gospel.

___ It's difficult for me to give my financial resources to my church.

___ I often serve others through church ministries.

___ My family and close friends know they can seek spiritual help from me.

___ Holiness is a major priority in my life.

Only God Knows

Whenever we take an inventory about our spiritual condition, we likely find room for growth. We often discover places where repentance is needed, proving that we're forgiven but not flawless. That's why active humility is important. God wants us to live out the transformation brought about in our lives by the gospel.

Humility desires God's leadership. But by seeking God's will, a humble Christian isn't just looking to obey marching orders but to draw close to the God who gives them. As we pursue holy lives, we do so not for the sake of the idea but for the sake of the One who's Sovereign Lord.

With that background let's look at how James guides us to seek God's will:

> Come now, you who say, "Today or tomorrow we will travel to such and such a city and spend a year there and do business and make a profit." Yet you do not know what tomorrow will bring—what your life will be! For you are like vapor that appears for a little while, then vanishes. Instead, you should say, "If the Lord wills, we will live and do this or that." But as it is, you boast in your arrogance. All such boasting is evil. So it is sin to know the good and yet not do it.
> **James 4:13-17**

What was the last major experience in your life that took you by surprise? How did it remind you of the brevity of life?

In the 1986 movie *Ferris Bueller's Day Off* the title character says, "Life moves pretty fast. If you don't stop and look around once in a while, you could miss it." The eccentric teenager convinces two friends to ditch school and go on an all-day adventure. Although the movie doesn't have a spiritual theme, the point should still resonate with Christians. Life is rapidly moving by, and we need to seize every moment, not with a self-centered, look-at-me, grab-what-I-can attitude but with the realization that life is coming at us, and we need to be prepared by knowing God's will for it.

Anyone can make few bucks here and there, travel around, and build a cool reputation. But God's plan for us is an active pursuit of humble holiness. It's not just a mental exercise. We must seek God's will and ways in this.

In many ways God's will is already revealed to us. By regularly reading the Bible, you receive the authoritative Word and will of God. His commands leap off the page and into our hearts. Then we're responsible for humbling ourselves to His will and joyfully responding in obedience.

> **Read these commands of Jesus and place an X beside the ones you're actively obeying.**
>
> ☐ Seek God's kingdom above all else (see Matt. 6:33).
> ☐ Be persistent in prayer (see Matt. 7:7-8).
> ☐ Take your burdens to Jesus (see Matt. 11:28).
> ☐ Take up your cross and follow Jesus (see Matt. 16:24).
> ☐ Forgive those who wrong you (see Matt. 18:21-22).
> ☐ Make disciples (see Matt. 28:18).
> ☐ Be at peace with one another (see Mark 9:50).
> ☐ Continue in His word (see John 8:31).
> ☐ Be a witness for the gospel (see Acts 1:8).

An emphasis on following God's will is good, but having an urgency for it is even better. Why? Because of the brevity of life. In comparison to eternity, our lives are just a vapor that's present for only a moment (see Jas. 4:14). Understanding the brevity of our lives will lead us to seek the eternal wisdom of our Creator. It's awe-inspiring to know that the God of eternity wants to guide the lives of mortals like us. He's interested. He loves. He wants to engage us in His work in this world in order to have an eternal impact on people who need Him. Humbling ourselves under His beautiful, perfect will is a vital part of pursuing holiness.

Boasting the Right Way

James leaves us with a warning against boasting. Knowing we have a tendency to take too much credit, he guides us away from evil arrogance and emphasizes God's sovereign will for our lives. This passage complements Paul's teaching to the Christians in Corinth:

> Brothers and sisters, consider your calling: Not many were wise from a human perspective, not many powerful, not many of noble birth. Instead, God has chosen what is foolish in the world to shame the wise, and God has chosen what is weak in the world to shame the strong. God has chosen what is insignificant and despised in the world—what is viewed as nothing—to bring to nothing what is viewed as something, so that no one may boast in his presence. It is from him that you are in Christ Jesus, who became wisdom from God for us—our righteousness, sanctification, and redemption, in order that, as it is written: Let the one who boasts, boast in the Lord.
> **1 Corinthians 1:26-31**

As you finish today's study, praise God for the following.
- The resurrection of Jesus
- God's work in your life to display His power, His wisdom, and His will
- God's great love for you

Spend time thanking God for every great blessing He has brought into your life over the past year. Give Him all the praise for the joy in your life because you're in Jesus Christ.

Powerful Lives
of Prayer

Week 6

Holiness can be pursued, but in the end it's a supernatural work that God completes in our lives. Therefore, focusing on prayer is an appropriate way to conclude our study of holiness.

Prayer has been defined in a multitude of ways. Martin Luther, the great Reformer of the church, once described prayer as "climbing up into the heart of God."[1] It's an action we take to both speak and listen to God as we worship Him and seek His help. Fisher Humphreys, one of my seminary professors, described prayer in class one day as "talking to God, who listens and responds because He loves us." Prayer is essentially our two-way communication with the King of glory.

Holiness is both something we've eternally inherited and something we pursue in this life. God has given us the gift of prayer as a vital means of seeking holiness. Like the pursuit of holiness itself, prayer aligns our hearts and our lives with Christ. It's a habit of holiness that shows our allegiance to our King.

We relationally connect with God through prayer. In the secret recesses of our hearts, we surrender all of our needs to Him. Through the regular practice of relational surrender, we can set our lives apart from selfish ambitions for God's kingdom purposes.

You've likely practiced prayer individually. Let's seek a life of prayer together so that we can pursue holiness as God's people.

---

1. Martin Luther, QuoteFancy.com, accessed September 8, 2017, https://quotefancy.com/quote/863882/Martin-Luther-Prayer-is-climbing-up-into-the-heart-of-God.

Start

Prayer is one of the greatest gifts that God has given us. It gives us immediate access to the Creator. In prayer we can be completely honest with God about the state of our heart and all of our needs.

What are some issues you've recently prayed about?

What subjects have your church and small group recently prayed about?

How did God respond to those prayers?

There are some common misconceptions about prayer. Some people use it as a Christian version of a good-luck charm: "If I pray, good things will happen." We must fight the temptation to treat prayer in a transactional manner. Prayer isn't a spiritual equation dictating that if we pray, we obligate God to do what we ask.

Prayer is one way we respond to the work of the gospel that has radically changed us. If you met a high-ranking leader of your company who gave you her personal cell-phone number, you wouldn't discard it. You would use it. The person of authority gave you private, personal access. However, you would never dream of using that access to make personal demands.

Prayer is our private, personal access to the Lord who leads us. Its purpose isn't to demand our way with Him. Its purpose is for Him to show His ways to us.

Pray that God will open your hearts and minds before you watch video session 6.

Watch

Use the space below to follow along and take notes as you watch video session 6.

When it comes to pursuing holiness, prayer is one of the most active portions of what you can do and who you can become.

Our prayers, offered together, help us to seek a life of holiness together.

When we pray together for needs—physical or spiritual—God is always attentive.

Prayer is the work where you align yourself with what God is doing.

James ends with a missional call.

Your pursuit of a holy life is for everybody around you—to help them to see that they can also walk fully in the power of Christ with the filling of the Spirit.

Discuss

Use the following statements and questions to discuss the video.

We're all busy people running from one chore to another, shuttling kids around, and trying to get ahead in life. The world tries to convince us that the busier we are, the more successful we'll be. But we usually end up tired rather than triumphant. We need a better way.

How can prayer provide needed relief from the crazy pace of life?

Read aloud James 5:13-15.

What are the most pressing prayer requests in your life?

We're taught to pray no matter what circumstance we encounter. Whether we suffer or rejoice, prayer is always the best choice. It's the path for us to place all of our needs before the God of the universe.

How could your church use prayer to encourage believers?

Prayer is an activity for individual believers and the corporate body of Christ. The church is directed to pray with its leaders for people who have physical needs. Praying for those in need reminds us and them that God is good and is available to offer grace for our needs.

How does prayer align your will with the will of God?

Prayer is an act of surrender. Though we ask for a lot of things in prayer, it must be done with the attitude that God has an answer and we'll wait for it. As we pray, we must remain ready to adjust our lives as God makes His will known to us.

Read aloud James 5:16-20.

How does your life of holiness relate to the effectiveness of your prayers?

Prayer can't be separated from the rest of our lives. Our conversations with God are an extension of the way we live the rest of our lives. And vice versa. Praying in faith and with a confessional attitude prepares us for God's work. As our holiness grows, our relational intimacy with God grows, and our prayers become more effective.

How does our call to missional work relate to our need for a prayer-filled life?

We're called to help people trapped in sin, but there's no way we'll naturally know how to do it. We need God's wisdom for working in God's mission. God is ready to give us insight if we'll ask for it.

Why does this letter from James about living a holy life end with a call to reach out to people trapped in sin?

James's letter naturally leads us from prayer to missional living. The pursuit of holiness is the desire to live by God's will and according to God's ways. It's His intention to save people from their sins, and we get to participate in that mission when we give Him total control of our lives.

Conclude the group session with the prayer activity on the following page.

Pray

Conclude the group session by praying for yourself and group members in specific ways. Here are some prayer priorities to focus on before the next group session.

- Love for Christ that exceeds the joy you find in anything else

- God's guidance about legitimate needs in your life, not wishes and preferences

- For the church to have a vibrant prayer life that consistently seeks God's wisdom and power

- For group members to be strengthened in their commitment to prayer

- Faithfulness to Bible study and to a consistent prayer life that will draw you closer to God

Prayer Requests

Decide what you'll study next as a group. Encourage members to complete "This Week's Plan" before the next time you meet.

This Week's Plan

Work with your group leader each week to create a plan for personal study, worship, and application between group sessions. Select from the following optional activities to match your personal preferences and available time.

Worship

[ ] Read your Bible. Complete the reading plan on page 110.

[ ] Spend time with God by engaging with the devotional experience on page 111.

[ ] Pray daily for the church and for group members.

Personal Study

[ ] Read and interact with "How We Pray Together" on page 112.

[ ] Read and interact with "Confession That Leads to Holiness" on page 116.

Application

[ ] Identify a topic of prayer you've been neglecting. Take time this week for focused prayers in that area.

[ ] Memorize James 5:16: "Confess your sins to one another and pray for one another, so that you may be healed. The prayer of a righteous person is very powerful in its effect."

[ ] Journal about a time when prayer was a great comfort in your life. Include your requests to God and the answers you received.

[ ] List five people you want to pray for daily during the next month. Let them know you're praying for them and ask them for prayer requests.

Did you miss the group session?
Video sessions available for purchase at lifeway.com/pursuingholiness

109

Read

Read the following Scripture passages this week. Use the acronym HEAR and the space provided to record your thoughts or action steps.

Day 1: Ephesians 3:16-19

Day 2: Matthew 6:5-15

Day 3: Philippians 1:9-11

Day 4: John 17:20-26

Day 5: Matthew 7:7-11

Day 6: Colossians 1:9-12

Day 7: Psalm 141:1-2

Reflect

PRAYING LIKE JESUS

Sometimes we wonder what's the best way to pray. Jesus' prayer in John 17 gives us excellent direction. Having entered Jerusalem the week before His crucifixion and delivered lengthy teaching in chapters 13–16, Jesus paused to pray.

The prayer in John 17 is often called the High Priestly prayer because Jesus served as both the High Priest and the Lamb of God. As our High Priest, He offered a sacrifice for sin. As the Lamb of God, He was the sacrifice for sin. His prayer reflects His desires for Himself and for His followers.

In the first section, verses 1-5, Jesus prayed for Himself. He asked the Father to glorify Him in the work that was to come—His death and resurrection. Jesus knew the time for ministry was over and the time for His atoning death had arrived.

In the second section, verses 6-19, Jesus prayed for the disciples who were alive at the time. He asked the Father not only to protect the believers but also to sanctify them with the Word. He knew they would have a dangerous path ahead that would require holiness.

In the final section, verses 20-26, Jesus prayed for us—all the Christians who would come after the firsthand witnesses of the Christ. Two major themes in this section are glory and unity. Jesus wants us to live for the glory of God and to be a showcase of His power for the rest of the world.

As we seek guidance for holiness, Jesus' prayer is a great place to look. It encourages us to live out our salvation regardless of the dangers posed by the world. God's glory is worth the risk, and the unity Jesus provides His body, the church, is a beautiful portrait of His salvation.

Personal Study 1

HOW WE PRAY TOGETHER

Prayer functions as both the most common and the most mysterious practice in the Christian life. At any moment we can communicate with God. Contemplate the power of that idea. Prayer is relational access to the God who not only created everything and holds everything together but also provided our salvation and rules over everything.

Prayer is an awesome gift. God uses it to direct our lives both individually and collectively as the church. Believers practice prayer on every relational level because it affects every relationship in our lives.

How would you describe the prayer life of your congregation?

Why Do We Pray?

Prayer centers on our relationship with God. Why do we talk and listen to people? Because information needs to be exchanged. But we prefer to talk with the people we love. We want to be involved in their lives, and we want them to be involved in our lives. Prayer is one way we can know the will of God and seek His intervention in our lives.

This foundational commitment to a relationship with God is the reason we mustn't allow selfishness to drive our prayer lives. We've already learned that James teaches us to seek holiness, tame our tongues, and persevere through trials. We do all this to put the character of Christ on display. Our prayer lives can do the same. Our prayers can put Christ first, even as we decide what priorities we'll pray for.

We engage in prayer not because we're trying to get what we want but because we want to desire the things God wants. Why? Because our desires often run amok from the values and priorities of the kingdom of God.

What issues do you find yourself praying about most often?

List problems in other people's lives that currently require your attention in prayer.

Whole prayer is pursuing the One who gives holiness, not being a demanding child who stamps his feet to get trinkets. As you complete this week's study, keep a humble spirit and allow the Lord to lead you to pray for the things He's passionate about. James identified some of those things:

Is anyone among you suffering? He should pray. Is anyone cheerful? He should sing praises. Is anyone among you sick? He should call for the elders of the church, and they are to pray over him, anointing him with oil in the name of the Lord. The prayer of faith will save the sick person, and the Lord will raise him up; if he has committed sins, he will be forgiven.
James 5:13-15

In what ways can the church pray for one another?

Praying with One Another

As we pray, we participate in others' lives at every level. We pray in their suffering, rejoicing, and sickness. Holy followers of Christ seek God in response to every experience that we or others encounter.

Turning to God in prayer is a distinctively Christian response. Think about ways people respond to a friend's suffering, joy, and sickness. They may display a passing interest in someone else's joy, but apathy or jealousy can also follow. That's why many companies have strict policies that restrict discussions of salaries. Most people can't be glad for coworkers who received a raise if they didn't receive one also. As we pursue holiness, we can more easily celebrate another person's joys, even if we weren't blessed in the same way. It's not a naïve response but an intentional decision to celebrate joy wherever we see it. Why? Because we know all good gifts come from the Heavenly Father (see Jas. 1:17).

James used the word *psallo* for *praises* at the end of verse 13. Similar to the name of the Old Testament Book of Psalms, the word refers to singing in worship. James was saying we should join people in prayer and praise to celebrate God's good work in their lives.

> **List some joys and celebrations that people in your small group are experiencing. Take time to praise God for their blessings.**

Prayer is also the way we respond to difficulties in other people's lives. In response to those suffering (see Jas. 5:13) and to those who are sick (see vv. 14-15), James used the word *proseuchomai*, the combination of two Greek words that literally mean "praying toward." It's the kind of prayer in which we beg God to intervene. We often call it intercessory prayer.

Make a list of the difficult circumstances that members of your small group are facing. Write *S, M, T, W, Th, F,* or *Sa* beside each need and commit to pray for it daily for the next week. Each day circle the letter to keep yourself accountable to pray for the need.

How can you develop more discipline to intercede for other people?

Praying for One Another

Praying for others involves much of what you've already learned about holiness. No wonder James included this teaching at the end of his letter. Allowing people to witness you at a weak point in your life will take mature perseverance, humility, reliance on heavenly wisdom, and faith. At this point of need, a believer's pursuit of holiness can be strengthened by the faith-filled prayers of the church.

In the example given by James, not only can sickness be relieved, but sins can also be forgiven. God can do both. He can perform a physical miracle to relieve suffering, and He can perform a spiritual miracle to relieve guilt. It's important to acknowledge that not all sick people get well. In fact, everyone eventually succumbs to the ultimate sickness—death. Nevertheless, God still directs us to seek Him in the trials of life because He's the only One who has the power to heal us and forgive our sin.

God is more aware of our needs than we are (see Isa. 65:24). One beautiful reminder of this truth is visible when the church gathers around the person in need. Christians can pray together rather than in solitude. The fellowship of the faithful is a signpost pointing to the God who knows our every need.

Personal Study 2

CONFESSION THAT LEADS TO HOLINESS

God has every intention of answering our prayers. That's why He gave us the gift of prayer. He uses prayer as a tool to draw us close to Himself and to guide us in His ways. We pursue a holy life with the assurance that God is bringing us into alignment with His character and His mission.

Read the following verses.

God has listened;
he has paid attention to the sound of my prayer.
Psalm 66:19

I will give thanks to you
because you have answered me
and have become my salvation.
Psalm 118:21

You will call to me and come and pray to me, and I will listen to you.
Jeremiah 29:12

Whatever you ask in my name, I will do it so that the Father may be glorified in the Son. If you ask me anything in my name, I will do it.
John 14:13-14

This is the confidence we have before him: If we ask anything according to his will, he hears us. And if we know that he hears whatever we ask, we know that we have what we have asked of him.
1 John 5:14-15

What does God's attentiveness to our prayers tell us about Him?

What's the key you see in these verses that allows us to receive what we request in prayer?

Living for the Answer

When you ask a question of another person, having to wait for the answer can be terrible. Whether it's a momentary hesitation or a delay of several days, you're held in suspense, just living for the answer. We obsess over it. We wait for it. Satisfaction is put on hold until we get the answer.

But what if living for the answer had a new meaning? Believers aren't just surviving until the answer comes. As we seek holiness, the way we live has an influence on when the answer arrives.

In all of the verses we read, the context and some of the language stipulate that the person praying lives by God's will and asks in the right spirit. The apostle John's words make this clear: make your petitions according to the will of God (see I John 5:14). When we ask for what God desires to provide through His perfect will, then we'll receive.

Aligning our actions, passions, and will with God's providential plans allows us to walk in holiness so that our desires are shaped by God's desires. Having the right spirit in prayer means the first request we ask of God is to know exactly what we should ask of Him. Then we're praying in the name, the power, and the reputation of Jesus. We're living in such a way that we can receive an answer.

Confess and Believe

The prayers of a holy person are made in faith. When we've made the leap that allows God to have complete rule over our lives, our prayers are accompanied by confidence in God's abilities.

Read these verses from James:

> Confess your sins to one another and pray for one another, so that you may be healed. The prayer of a righteous person is very powerful in its effect. Elijah was a human being as we are, and he prayed earnestly that it would not rain, and for three years and six months it did not rain on the land. Then he prayed again, and the sky gave rain and the land produced its fruit.
> **James 5:16-18**

What issues does James direct us to pray about? List specific illustrations of each one in your life.

We pursue holiness only if we're desperate. It's not a small matter to want a life that's utterly different from what we currently have. This fact highlights another role of prayer. When we confess sin, we're agreeing with God about what's true and right. Confession signals that our will has changed and that we're ready to turn around. When we desperately cry to God for forgiveness and restoration, we receive His righteousness through faith. That's the reason such a prayer is powerful and effective. It's not that the person praying is great. It's that the God being prayed to is great.

Elijah knew God's power and greatness. First Kings 17–19 records many ways God answered his prayers and worked through him. James wrote that he was a normal guy just like the rest of us. But Elijah prayed for God to do powerful signs, and the Lord answered. He showed a deep reliance on God, and he received answers to his prayers.

Prayer doesn't require any special skills. A life of faith centers on what God has done, can do, and will do. It's never about what we can accomplish by our wit and wisdom. We're limited by what we can put our hands on and put our minds to. God's limitless power allows Him to transcend anything we think is possible. That includes providing rain in a drought and forgiving the sins of a wayward follower.

> **Rank yourself by responding to the following statements, with 1 being completely apathetic and 5 being completely passionate.**
> ___ I'm desperate for God's presence in my life.
> ___ I believe God wants to answer my prayers.
> ___ I'll submit all of my daily decisions to God in prayer.
> ___ I have faith that God can meet the needs in my life.
> ___ When my needs aren't met, I look to God for insight.

Elijah offered his prayers in faith because of his confidence in the character of God. That confidence came from having faithfully walked with God for a long time. Because Elijah had already witnessed God's abilities to answer people's needs, he was willing to confess God's sovereignty over his life and his circumstances.

Elijah was like many other saints throughout the Bible who offered their lives to God first and then sought God's intervention in their circumstances. Their confessions preceded their requests. When they demonstrated holiness, their prayers were made effective.

> **Before you make any new requests to God, first ask the Holy Spirit whether you're walking in holiness. Respond to His leading.**

Leader Guide

Opening and Closing Group Sessions

Always try to engage with each person at the beginning of the group session. Once a person speaks, even if only to answer a generic question, he or she is more likely to speak up later about more personal matters.

You may want to begin each session by reviewing the previous week's personal study. This review provides context for the new session and opportunities to share relevant experiences, application, or biblical truths learned between sessions. Then set up the theme of the session's group study to prepare personal expectations.

Always open and close the session with prayer, recognizing that only the Holy Spirit provides understanding and transformation in our lives. The prayer suggestions provided in each session help members focus on Scripture, key truths, and personal application from the week's teaching.

Remember that the goal isn't just meaningful discussion but discipleship.

SESSION 1

Wise and Humble Endurance

Summary statements help clarify key teaching points and provide direction for the questions that follow. (You'll make summary statements several times in each session.)

Always keep God's Word central during the group discussion. Ultimately, you want participants to hear what God says. Asking someone to read Scripture can engage more people in the topic of study.

What have been your usual definitions or ways of thinking about the concept of holiness?

Establishing a common understanding of holiness is important for the entire study. It's important to listen to group members' ideas even if they seem to be distant from a biblical understanding. Knowing their level of understanding will help you lead the group more effectively.

How would a more extensive definition of *holiness* change the way you relate to Jesus?

How can we turn our trials into joyful experiences?

In what areas of life—trials, temptations, or victories—do you need to seek God's wisdom to better understand your circumstances?

This question will require openness from a group member to start the conversation. You may choose to ask someone before the group session to be prepared to answer the question.

How can you make a deeper connection in your life between hearing the Word and obeying it?

What's one way you need to obey God's Word this week?

Why do faith and good works operate as companions for Christians?

Be prepared to answer questions about the nature of salvation. When reading James, people can become confused and think he was addressing the way we're saved. If that's the case, someone could mistakenly believe that we're saved by our works. Your role will be to clarify that our works demonstrate that we've already been saved.

> **Describe a current circumstance in your life that requires faithful waiting and endurance.**
>
> **What changes would you like Jesus to make in your life in order to be glorified in you?**

These questions help the group apply the truth. As the leader, guide the discussion to move from ideas to actions.

Concluding your discussion with personal-application questions is important. Help group members adopt action steps for applying the truth to their daily lives. Sharing your own personal experiences will accomplish this task.

Before you conclude in prayer, ask for members' final input or questions. This gives members an opportunity to share thoughts or ask questions that may not have been considered during the discussion. It creates an environment of openness and shared ownership of the group session by showing that everyone's input is valued.

SESSION 2

Obedience in Real Time

The religious background of group members has a powerful impact on the way they process the Scriptures and the group discussions. Obedience can be a concept some struggle with for various reasons. If they have a legalistic background, they may seek a set of rules to fulfill. If they have a nonreligious background, they might struggle with the idea of living within the boundary markers outlined for a holy life.

It's critical for you, as the group leader, to understand the lives of the members. As appropriate, have personal conversations with group members so that you'll understand their personal histories and spiritual conditions.

What's the danger of making holiness just a mental exercise?

Some people participate in every Bible study offered by the church because they like learning. Help members accept the idea that holiness includes our thinking but doesn't end with it.

What would make the biggest difference in helping you move from hearing the truth to acting on the truth?

What's the danger of spending time learning the Word without any intention of obeying it?

Discussing the world's deceitfulness can dredge up very negative emotions. People can feel shame or embarrassment for things they've done. Allow people to express these emotions; then convey God's grace to them.

What are some modern examples of exercising the type of faith that James 1:27 commends?

As the leader, make sure you've read all the weeks' personal studies and viewed all the videos so that you can guide the group effectively.

Compare your own faith to the demonic faith that James described (see Jas. 2:19). How does that statement challenge you?

What's a biblical lesson that's often taught but seems to be difficult for many believers to obey? What makes obedience difficult?

In answering some questions, group members may want to give negative statements about specific people. Guide them to speak about their personal lives, as well as ways they can help others walk faithfully with Christ.

How do the characters of Abraham and Rahab differ? What was the common characteristic they shared?

With some questions you're asking members to talk about their personal histories. There are no right or wrong answers when people reflect their own experiences. The important factor is that you help them incorporate biblical truth into their understandings of their experiences in the past and in their current circumstances. Asking a question about the biblical text after personal questions helps them make important connections. Even though their emotions may vary as they make application, you can help the whole group support people as they move through this process.

Before you conclude in prayer, ask for members' final input or questions. This gives members an opportunity to share thoughts or ask questions that may not have been considered during the discussion. It creates an environment of openness and shared ownership of the group session by showing that everyone's input is valued.

SESSION 3

Relationships of Grace

Group leaders need to have an awareness of current events in the lives of group members. Before having this week's session, take time to contact members in ways that are convenient for them (phone call, text message, social media, etc.) and ask how they feel the study is aiding their spiritual journeys. Knowing how they're dealing with current circumstances of life will give you insight to prepare more effectively as their leader.

Because this session focuses on relationships, realize that some members may offer emotional answers to the questions. Remember that everyone needs a safe place to express their emotions and that Bible-study times are opportunities to direct those emotions properly.

What types of people are the most difficult to be around and express your faith in Jesus?

What should be a church's normal reaction to someone who seems out of place in a worship service?

Questions about ways people are treated by a congregation can cause members to digress with their answers. Be prepared to help the group get back on track when they begin to wander into other topics of discussion.

How can a church actively work to eliminate favoritism in its relationships?

With questions about church life, help members steer away from turning the discussion into a gripe session. Ask them for constructive comments.

Why do we surrender to the temptation of favoring the powerful of the world instead of valuing the poor?

What does it mean to love someone else "as yourself" (Jas. 2:8)?

Asking open-ended questions will allow for more robust discussion. Avoid yes-or-no questions that will inhibit further discussion of a topic. Even with open-ended questions, encourage the person who answers to elaborate further on the response. Your goal is to help members fully process how biblical truth can apply many ways in their lives.

How would living by God's will and ways display holiness in our relationships with others?

What practical steps can you take to change from a perspective of judgment to a perspective of mercy?

Asking questions that evoke a testimony, a story, or an emotion is a powerful way to help group members connect with one another. These questions also encourage members to share ways they struggle to apply biblical principles to real-life situations. As the leader, you can then guide the group to offer encouragement to one another.

Before you conclude in prayer, ask for members' final input or questions. This gives members an opportunity to share thoughts or ask questions that may not have been considered during the discussion. It creates an environment of openness and shared ownership of the group session by showing that everyone's input is valued.

SESSION 4
Putting Holiness into Practice

The past experiences of group members have a powerful impact on their current beliefs. In preparing for this session, consider past experiences in your life. As you think about practical ways to live a holy life, delve into experiences that advanced your maturity in Christ and temptations that stood in the way. When dealing with how we speak to one another and the wisdom we use for daily decisions, be authentic about your own struggles.

What habits help you get through a tough day?

The word *habit* normally has a negative undertone. In this instance you're trying to help group members think about making holiness a habitual, normal practice in their lives. Let them work through the process of transforming the idea of habit from negative to positive.

What are some common ways people stumble by using their words poorly?

Personal stories from group members powerfully communicate the way God works through His Word and in His church. Prepare the group for success by calling a group member ahead of the session and asking him or her to answer one of the first questions to spark conversation in the group.

What do the images of horses, boats, and fire contribute to your understanding of the power of the tongue?

What causes you to lose control and speak poorly to other people?

How do the worldly motivations of hoarding things, achieving more, and gaining a reputation contribute to an unholy life?

People need proper motivations for living faithfully. Help the group compare the worldly motivations for success of hoarding, achievements, and reputation and the godly motivations of kingdom, covenant, and fellowship. Find examples of ways Scripture describes believers' motivations and ways they differ from temptations.

What descriptor of holy living in James 3:17 needs attention in your life?

How can you actively help and pray for group members to pursue holiness more effectively?

Always help members move from theoretical answers to practical actions they can take.

Before you conclude in prayer, ask for members' final input or questions. This gives members an opportunity to share thoughts or ask questions that may not have been considered during the discussion. It creates an environment of openness and shared ownership of the group session by showing that everyone's input is valued.

SESSION 5
The Way of Humility

The purpose of the group session is to have an honest discussion about biblical truth that will be applied to the Christian life on a daily basis. When you sense that group members are growing resistant to participate, talk with them individually to discover what's happening. They may be dealing with new, difficult problems in life, or the subject of the session may be particularly convicting for them. Never assume the worst about group members when they grow quiet over time. Instead, use these opportunities to minister to members' needs.

> **When you were a kid, what was the most common reason for arguments and fights with your friends?**

Some members are hesitant to discuss their childhoods. The reasons can range from mere timidity to trauma associated with abuse. If someone doesn't have a childhood story, don't point them out or make a joke. Simply allow people to share on a level that's comfortable for them.

> **What's an occasion when Jesus showed great humility?**

Asking group members to recall another part of the Bible may prove challenging to people who are new to studying Scripture. Be prepared to give multiple examples from Jesus' life that illustrate the point. Another approach is to give each member a passage to read silently for a few minutes and then have each person give a short overview of the story from Jesus' life.

> **How will choosing to serve propel your pursuit of holiness?**

Help members learn how different biblical ideas relate to one another. This study of holiness is leading believers to integrate the concept of holiness with all aspects of doctrine and life. Therefore, prepare for the natural questions about how these ideas relate to one another. As the group leader, learn to anticipate the possible objections that may arise.

How does humbling ourselves before God relate to the way we treat other people?

How often do you think about the hereafter? How do those thoughts affect the way you make daily decisions?

With questions about how people generally think or act, do some research before the group session to find reliable information. Utilize reputable research groups or studies to help you lead the discussion.

Before you conclude in prayer, ask for members' final input or questions. This gives members an opportunity to share thoughts or ask questions that may not have been considered during the discussion. It creates an environment of openness and shared ownership of the group session by showing that everyone's input is valued.

SESSION 6
Powerful Lives of Prayer

Prayer is a concept that spans many major religions and philosophies. It's also understood differently in various Christian denominations and traditions. As you prepare to lead the discussion of prayer, consider group members' religious or nonreligious backgrounds. Try to anticipate what their reactions to this discussion will be so that you can guide the conversation to focus on a biblical view of prayer.

How can prayer provide needed relief from the crazy pace of life?

What are the most pressing prayer requests in your life?

Asking for prayer requests can open the conversation for people to admit doubts and fears. Craft your responses to any verbalized doubts to communicate grace and sympathy. Members should feel that it's safe to confess their dire need for God to provide relief.

How could your church use prayer to encourage believers?

Keep a positive attitude when discussing your church. Members will take their cues from you or from the strongest personality in the group. Don't allow personal insults to persist in the discussion if a weakness about the church is highlighted. Instead, ask the group to identify ways the church can become stronger in any challenging areas that are raised.

How does prayer align your will with the will of God?

How does your life of holiness relate to the effectiveness of your prayers?

Questions about the character and work of God are critical to the core of your discussions. Holiness isn't just about being the most moral person in the neighborhood but allowing God to direct every part of your life. As you discuss the will of God, allow members to search for a deeper understanding of His character.

How does our call to missional work relate to our need of a prayer-filled life?

Why does this letter from James about living a holy life end with a call to reach out to people trapped in sin?

End the study on a positive note. Ask members to identify the major learning points and their responses to what they have learned. Allow time for members to share ways the study has adjusted their thinking and is guiding new ways of living.

Before you conclude in prayer, ask for members' final input or questions. This gives members an opportunity to share thoughts or ask questions that may not have been considered during the discussion. It creates an environment of openness and shared ownership of the group session by showing that everyone's input is valued.

Tips for Leading a Small Group

Prayerfully Prepare

Prepare for each group session with prayer. Ask the Holy Spirit to work through you and the group discussion as you point to Jesus each week through God's Word.

REVIEW the weekly material and group questions ahead of time.

PRAY for each person in the group.

Minimize Distractions

Do everything in your ability to help people focus on what's most important: connecting with God, with the Bible, and with one another. Create a comfortable environment. If group members are uncomfortable, they'll be distracted and therefore not engaged in the group experience. Take into consideration seating, temperature, lighting, refreshments, surrounding noise, and general cleanliness.

At best, thoughtfulness and hospitality show guests and group members they're welcome and valued in whatever environment you choose to gather. At worst, people may never notice your effort, but they're also not distracted.

Include Others

Your goal is to foster a community in which people are welcome just as they are but encouraged to grow spiritually. Always be aware of opportunities to include and invite.

INCLUDE anyone who visits the group.

INVITE new people to join your group.

Encourage Discussion

A good small-group experience has the following characteristics.

EVERYONE PARTICIPATES. Encourage everyone to ask questions, share responses, or read aloud.

NO ONE DOMINATES—NOT EVEN THE LEADER. Be sure your time speaking as a leader takes up less than half your time together as a group. Politely guide discussion if anyone dominates.

NOBODY IS RUSHED THROUGH QUESTIONS. Don't feel that a moment of silence is a bad thing. People often need time to think about their responses to questions they've just heard or to gain courage to share what God is stirring in their hearts.

INPUT IS AFFIRMED AND FOLLOWED UP. Make sure you point out something true or helpful in a response. Don't just move on. Build community with follow-up questions, asking how other people have experienced similar things or how a truth has shaped their understanding of God and the Scripture you're studying. People are less likely to speak up if they fear that you don't actually want to hear their answers or that you're looking for only a certain answer.

GOD AND HIS WORD ARE CENTRAL. Opinions and experiences can be helpful, but God has given us the truth. Trust Scripture to be the authority and God's Spirit to work in people's lives. You can't change anyone, but God can. Continually point people to the Word and to active steps of faith.

Keep Connecting

Think of ways to connect with group members during the week. Participation during the group session is always improved when members spend time connecting with one another outside the group sessions. The more people are comfortable with and involved in one another's lives, the more they'll look forward to being together. When people move beyond being friendly to truly being friends who form a community, they come to each session eager to engage instead of merely attending.

Encourage group members with thoughts, commitments, or questions from the session by connecting through emails, texts, and social media.

Build deeper friendships by planning or spontaneously inviting group members to join you outside your regularly scheduled group time for meals; fun activities; and projects around your home, church, or community.

Group Information

NAME   **CONTACT**

DISCIPLE FOR LIFE

The Disciple for Life series emphasizes modeling and practice without compromising biblical knowledge or redemptive community. Developed for groups of as few as two people (or more), each study includes short videos, a leader guide that identifies core principles and elements of effective small-group leadership, and of course, content for growing as a disciple for life.

BASICS
Understanding the Foundations of a Healthy Church
6 sessions

Get a comprehensive understanding of the church and its organization and practices.

Bible Study Book 006104044 $12.99
Leader Kit 006104045 $39.99

KNOWING JESUS
Living by His Name
6 sessions

Move toward a more intimate relationship with Jesus through His miracles, what He said about Himself, and what others said about Him.

Bible Study Book 005791554 $12.99
Leader Kit 005791555 $39.99

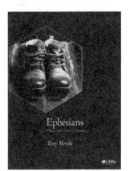

EPHESIANS
Your Identity in Christ
6 sessions

Get practical answers to contemporary believers' basic questions about the Christian life.

Bible Study Book 005792212 $12.99
Leader Kit 005792213 $39.99